PIER LUIGI NERVI

PIER LUIGI NERVI

Tullia Iori

Motta Architettura

Pier Luigi Nervi

Cover
Palazzo del Lavoro, Turin
Photo

Translation
Soget srl

minimum
essential architecture library

Series edited by Giovanni Leoni

Published Titles

Santiago Calatrava
Richard Meier
Álvaro Siza

For the excerpts reproduced in the sections "Thought" and "Critique," the authors and publishers wish to thank those who have authorised their publication. The publisher is available for any queries regarding sections for which it has not been possible to trace the holder of the rights.

First edition: March 2009

ISBN: 978-88-6413-005-7

Printed in Italy

Contents

Portfolio

INGRESSO 7

Introduction

Pier Luigi Nervi: engineer, architect, builder

In 1960 Pier Luigi Nervi was the most famous engineer in the world. His most recent structures, designed to host the events of the Rome Olympic Games, had been published in the world's most authoritative technical publications and had earned him a Royal Gold Medal, the world's most prestigious architecture award at the time[1].
During the Games, broadcast on more than 100 television channels throughout Europe and the United States, the cantilever roof of Flaminio stadium and the domes of the Palazzo e del Palazzetto dello Sport served as backdrop for legendary sporting events. The structures were unanimously recognised as masterpieces.
Nervi not only ideated the design projects (assisted by his eldest son Antonio, an architect, and a few trusted assistants), but he also presented irresistible offers that won him contracts for tenders for building them, which he did though his small family-run construction company, Ingg. Nervi & Bartoli (his partner was his cousin). It took only four years from initial conception to construction.
How did he succeed in this exceptional enterprise, in a climate such as the one that pervaded Italy at that time, where delays were an ordinary part of the construction industry despite the economic boom? What form does his originality take?
Nervi's works are entirely Italian: containing no imitation of international models, they are the product of a long, intense, difficult process of architectural, static and constructive experimentation which the engineer had been working on for decades and which was, in subsequent years, to produce one of the most effective expressions of Italian style in the world.
The "Nervi system" is based on two original inventions[2]: a material, ferrocement, and a construction process, structural prefabrication. Patented before the end of the Second World War, during the difficult years of autarchy, this process had been perfected at the end of the war by application and fine-tuning of numerous projects during the Reconstruction.
To understand the construction successes of the 1960s, it is essential to retrace the precedents leading to this exploit.

A life dedicated to reinforced concrete

Pier Luigi Nervi's story is linked to reinforced concrete right from the start. He was born in 1891 in Sondrio, of Ligurian parents, one year before François Hennebique, the pioneer of reinforced concrete, filed his patent in France and Italy.
In 1913, after graduating with a degree in civil engineering from the Scuola di Applicazione in Bologna, Nervi worked for the Società Anonima per Costruzioni Cementizie under the guidance of his technical architecture professor, Attilio Muggia, who was the licensee for the Hennebique patent in central Italy. War soon interrupted his apprenticeship. Between 1915 and 1918 Nervi served in the Corps of Engineers (where he gained recognition for a series of inventions culminating in the idea of a hydrogen motor for missiles!). Once discharged, he resumed his work for the company and was assigned to its Florence offices, where he was given more and more responsibilities. His many reinforced concrete works, designed, calculated and overseen as supervisor of works at this time, consolidate his status as a mature, independent professional, and in 1923, when about to get married, he took the risk of leaving his secure employment to work for himself.
Nervi moved to Rome and founded his own company, Ing. Nervi & Nebbiosi, with entrepreneur and sole financier Rodolfo Nebbiosi. Finally free to choose and optimise his compositional and building systems, Nervi created his first original oversize roofs: Politeama Bruno Banchini in Prato (1923-1925) and Teatro Augusteo in Naples (1926-1929). But the catalogue of the company's projects also includes warehouses, industrial plants, tanks, and every possible kind of industrial or service building, the first structures in which reinforced concrete techniques were used. In 1928 he built the elegant building on Lungotevere Arnaldo da Brescia, designed by architect Giuseppe Capponi, which became his home and studio for the rest of his life. At the heart of the house is a spiral staircase, winding continuously from the entrance

opposite page
Construction site for a geodetic aircraft hangar in the second series, 1939

[1] In the years immediately prior, the award had been conferred upon Le Corbusier, Walter Gropius, Alvar Aalto and Mies van der Rohe.
[2] Nervi filed dozens of industrial patents over the course of his career, primarily in the field of construction, but also in other sectors.

Teatro Augusteo, view of construction site, Naples, 1926

opposite page
View of the construction site for one of the first series of geodetic aircraft hangars, 1935;
skeleton of one of the second series of aircraft hangars, 1939;
Nervi's 1939 patent for the structural prefabrication technique

hall to the attic in a contemporary interplay between dynamism and chromatics.
When he started designing Florence Stadium (1930-1933), the oeuvre sectioned into lots, which earned him international acclaim, Nervi broke with Nebbiosi. He elected to create a new, more independent company, founding Nervi & Bartoli in 1932.
The stadium, like the building that became his home, was greatly admired by Italian and international critics alike. They praised the project for the bold design of the cantilever roof and the winding curve of the stairways, an innovative aspect, capable of revolutionising the eclecticism that had become rather tedious and overdone. In the years to come, Nervi would continue working on functional structures without pause, also nurturing his relationship with young rationalist architects, participating in their exhibitions and publishing in avant-garde magazines. This is the time of his humorous studies of futuristic constructions (a floating hotel with a patented device to make it insensitive to the motion of the waves; a building that rotates to follow the sun; a monument to the flag, a 250-metre tower supported by a heavy internal pendulum hanging from the top) and his entries in major architecture competitions (especially the 1939 competition for the Palazzo dell'Acqua e della Luce for the E42).
But these were hard times for a designer and builder with so much experience with reinforced concrete. In 1937 the material was accused of not being "Italian" enough, and its use was first restricted to certain specific types of buildings and then, in 1939, banned.
What had happened? In 1935 Italy had invaded Ethiopia and the League of Nations had imposed heavy sanctions: no state was to sell materials to Italy that could be used by the war industry, particularly metals.
The regime profited from this opportunity to promote autarchy, that is, an economic self-sufficiency, which was in actual fact already intrinsic to the corporatist economic policy it had been implementing for years. At this critical time, the country's own modest steel production was obligatorily destined for exclusive use for armaments. The construction industry was obliged to relinquish steel rods and, consequently, reinforced concrete.
These difficulties encouraged Nervi's ingeniousness and experimentation. By then almost fifty years of age, with four small children, he found himself having to start all over again with a new form of design and construction (the second of three, as Sergio Poretti recently wrote)[3].

[3] S. Poretti, "Nervi che visse tre volte", in T. Iori, S. Poretti, *Pier Luigi Nervi. L'Ambasciata d'Italia a Brasilia*, Milan: Electa, 2008, pp. 8-49.

The invention of "ferrocement" and of "structural prefabrication"

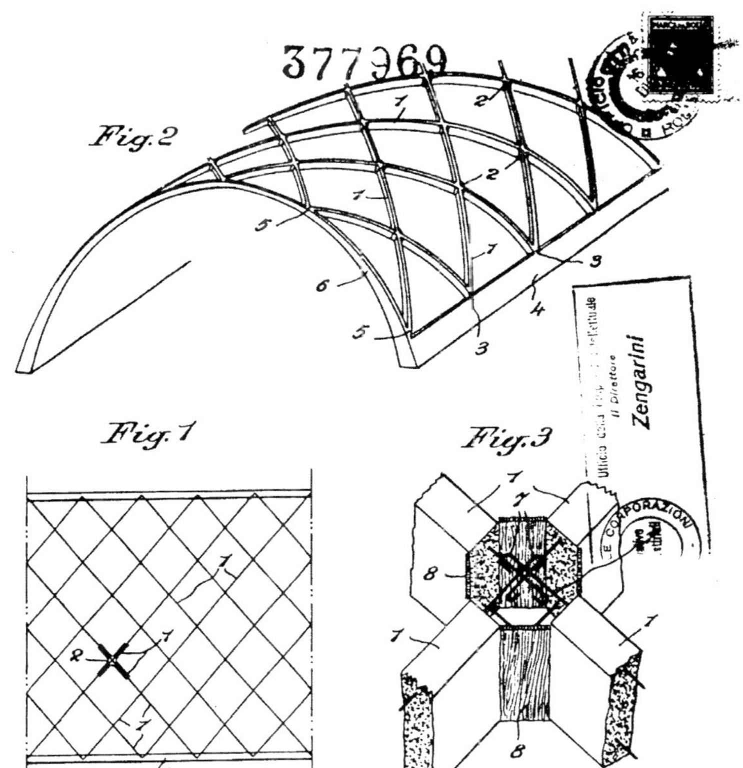

An opportunity to completely renew the reinforced concrete construction technique in which he had become a specialist was unconsciously offered by the young military Aeronautic Direction, which needed lots of hangars to protect its fleets for the war (and was of course allowed to use the prohibited anti-autarchic materials). This new type of building, though not subjected to any stylistic restrictions, had to have the possibly of being identically replicated in different airfields. This inspired Nervi to contrive some original construction solutions. The first series of two hangars with a geodetic structure for Orvieto airport (1935-1938) is made of reinforced concrete cast on site. The technique used in subsequent series (the most famous of which were also in Orvieto, Orbetello and Torre del Lago Puccini, though many others were built all over Italy), though practically the same in form, was patented in 1939 under the name "structural prefabrication." To attain this, Nervi broke down the structure into small, lightweight pieces that could easily be lifted and moved by workers and could thereby be replicated most anywhere.
The pieces were prefabricated on the ground, under shelters to protect them from the weather, and then, with their protruding rods, placed in their final position on the scaffolding and linked by casting a node with strong cement once they were in position. Following assemblage, the structure returned to a monolithic form. This simple yet efficient technique can be applied to all types of buildings (though it works best where there is an axis of symmetry) to save time and materials and, most important, expensive lumber.
It was while designing hangars that Nervi realised that his structures were often impossible to calculate statically, but he never shied away from complex forms if they were structurally valid. On the contrary, he requested the assistance of Arturo Danusso, a professor at Milan Polytechnic, to create scale models of the works he studied. These served to simulate loads and verify static behaviour. The model turned out to be a valuable tool, which Nervi avidly used until the end of his career.
But war had broken out and a stall in construction prevented him from experimenting with "decomposition" in other types of buildings. Nonetheless, Nervi never stopped contemplating

Ferrocement pavilion under construction at Magliana, Rome, 1945

the as yet unexpressed potential of reinforced concrete and his cerebral endeavours culminated in an innovative variant that he patented in April 1943. It was baptised ferrocement.

A brief explanation of what this material is follows. Ordinary reinforced concrete consists of a lot of cement conglomerate and a little bit of steel. A rectangular beam, for example, consists mainly of conglomerate, which is highly resistant to compression and reinforced with relatively few steel bars, making it resistant to traction. In his ferrocement, Nervi inverted the usual proportions of the two components, preparing a package of layered steel meshes, which he then covered with conglomerate, spreading it with a trowel from one side until the felt was saturated with mix so that it came out the other side, where it was finally smoothed off. The resulting slab was very thin, normally only three centimetres, but highly resistant, elastic, flexible and inexpensive (above all because it did not require formworks). Moreover, Nervi demonstrated that with the same span, his material, thanks to its reduced thickness, required much less steel than ordinary reinforced concrete.

Of course, in order to be useful in construction, ferrocement had to be formed into appropriate shapes (wavy or pleated, for example) to make it "resistant in shape" (like a thin sheet of paper capable of supporting a weight if "pleated").

In September 1943, after the armistice, the Nazis invaded Rome and Nervi closed down his business so that he would not be forced to collaborate, and retired into his home. His son Vittorio says that he used to hide young persecuted students who in shelters that he quickly fabricated created behind walls in his kitchen. His ferrocement slabs lay still on his balcony, where he thus tested their reaction to exposure to atmospheric agents. Rome was liberated in June 1944 and by the end of September Nervi had a new patent ready, perfected with all he had learnt in months of forced inactivity. He reopened his company and immediately built a small warehouse on his land in Magliana, made entirely of ferrocement (including the roof), three centimetres thick, shaped in waves

Ferrocement felt, 1943

to ensure the necessary stability. The warehouse is still there today to testify to the value of his invention, though it is improperly used and neglected.
To celebrate the end of the war, in May 1945 Nervi published a book he had been working on for some time. Titled *Scienza o arte del costruire?*, the text summarily recounted his experience with construction and optimistically estimated the resources of his innovations.
His career gradually took off again, mutedly: first his highly positive application of ferrocement to boats (motorboats, fishing boats, pontoons, the ketch Nennele – on which he continued to work for many years – and some vessels for the FAO). Lster, he concentrated on more and more difficult building prototypes, continually experimenting and perfecting his technique.
One day, he was finally given the opportunity to apply the system to a major work at the Salone B at the Torino Esposizioni. He built the roof in just a few months, between 1947 and the end of 1948, thanks to joint use of structural prefabrication and ferrocement, used to make the lightweight pieces into which the gigantic structure is broken down. Patented in 1948 and 1950 respectively, the "wave blocks" and the "hollow flat blocks" were to underlie all of Nervi's subsequent projects. The shaping of the pieces (waves or flat blocks) was achieved through a sequence of operations one might define "generational." A form made of earth or brick (referred to as the "grandmother"), smoothed with chalk, was used to make a sample (the "mother"), which was then turned upside-down and repeatedly used as a counter-form for preparation of several "daughter" elements, identical to the "grandmother," used for assembling the structure.
The space inside Hall B evokes a powerful sensation, which critics could not fail to note, especially foreign critics, amazed to see that a country that had been destroyed by war and worn away by twenty years of dictatorship could embark on such a bold, effective enterprise.
From that time on Nervi's career was in crescendo[4]. Beginning with the swimming pool at the Naval Academy in Livorno (1949) he then developed: the "La Tebaide" docks in San Michele di Pagana (1949); the Tobacco Workshop in Bologna (1949); Hall C, which completed the exhibition areas volumes in Turin (1950), the Salt Warehouses in Tortona (1950); the restaurant and trampoline in the Kursaal resort in Ostia (1950), the Gatti wool mill (1951), a minor masterpiece based on another of Nervi's inventions; the "isostatic ribbed ceiling, the party room in the spa in Chianciano (1952); and the tram deposit in Turin (1954).
These works completed in the early 1950s are almost always neglected in favour of the most complicated, well-known projects that came right after them, at the time when Nervi procuced most of his masterpieces: the Unesco offices in Paris (1952-1958), his first projects abroad, which established his reputation as Italy's most prestigious architect (linked with his collaboration on the CNIT); the Pirelli skyscraper in Milan (1955-1960), studied with Danusso; the Palazzetto

[4] For information on the co-designers and partners who worked with Nervi on projects in Italy and abroad mentioned here, refer to the chronologies and information sheets in this volume.

Construction of the Palazzo dello Sport, Rome, 1959, detail of floor with isostatic ribbing

[5] "Pier Luigi Nervi", in *Rassegna critica di Architettura*, edited by G. Perugini, 30, 1954; G.C. Argan, *Pier Luigi Nervi*, Milan: Il Balcone, 1955 (published in Spanish in the same year by Infinito of Buenos Aires).
[6] *Pier Luigi Nervi*, Milan: Edizioni di Comunità, 1957 (with a preface by P.L. Nervi, an introduction by E.N. Rogers and explanatory notes to the illustrations by J. Joedicke), also published in French, German and English in the same year.

(1956-1957) and Palazzo dello Sport (1956-1959) in Rome; the Corso Francia viaduct (1959), raised on pillars which change shape as they rise upwards (another statically optimal invention, very easy to obtain in construction but extraordinarily effective in formal terms); Flaminio Stadium (1956-1959), the first occasion on which his son Antonio, who graduated in 1950 and had already been helping him for some years, was officially presented as his partner. As the Games opened, Nervi was already at work on the Palazzo del Lavoro in Turin (1959-1961), destined to host the most important exhibition celebrating the centennial of the unification of Italy, and the suspended structure of Burgo Paper Mill in Mantua (1960-1964).
The fine tuning of the "Nervi method" was aided by the apparently unstoppable ferment of construction that led the country through the hard times of reconstruction and into an economic boom. Italy was building, and Nervi, though well-known and authoritative, was not an isolated case. A large group of structural architects (including Riccardo Morandi, Sergio Musmeci and Silvano Zorzi, among many others) was rising to international success thanks in part to a tough programme of public works financed during the presidency of Giovanni Gronchi (between 1956 and 1964, these included the Autostrada del Sole motorway, immediately recognised as a masterpiece of engineering).

The Nervi method rises to international success

Nervi received many awards starting in the fifties, and his first honorary degree, from the Faculty of Architecture of Buenos Aires University, was only the first of many others. His first monographs

appeared in 1954, initially published only in Italian[5], then translated into major languages.6 In 1955 Nervi published *Costruire correttamente*, 7 in which he personally presented his ideas and projects. In the early sixties, the successes of the economic boom were accompanied not only by thousands of articles published in specialised and general publications in Italy and abroad, but by new monographs,8 exhibitions and honours,9 as well as the last of his books, *Nuove strutture*, 10 published in 1963.
In the meantime, Studio Nervi was founded, with Pier Luigi and Antonio collaborating (with the addition of two more sons, Mario and Vittorio, in 1960), in a design workshop kept clearly separate from the construction firm.
Unfortunately, Italy's economic boom gave way to recession in 1963. The crisis, which initially seemed temporary, worsened and drove the country into the "Years of Lead." While Nervi & Bartoli immediately felt the impact of the economic crisis, the design studio took advantage of its fame to find work all over the world, forming partnerships with other important local architects or independently designing structures translating the themes typical of the "Nervi method" into an international architectural vocabulary.
The New York bus station (1961-1962), St. Mary's Cathedral in San Francisco (1966-1971), the structures for the Stock Exchange Tower in Montreal, Canada (1962-1966) or the Australia Tower in Sydney (1961-1967), the Italian Embassy in Brasilia (1969-1976) and the Good Hope Centre in Cape Town, South Africa (1970-1978) are only a few of a long list of intercontinental projects flanked by dozens of plans (including a 1969 for a bridge over the Strait of Messina, for the competition ambitiously promoted by the Italian government).
In this new role as international designer, Nervi could not be the builder too (his company was too small to compete with big foreign enterprises) and so these works lost an essential component, the masterful and expert building technique that set apart exclusive products from those that are mass-produced. This, however, was an essential decision. Nervi the designer, used to ideating his own projects and then personally overseeing their construction, had to move on, to develop a line, or a brand, for the global market, even while retaining his originality and recognisability. Nervi's reputation is based on domes and vaults with triangular or diamond-shaped hollow flat blocks, on ceilings with isostatic ribbing, on pillars of variable shape. He not only rose to success all over the world, but helped consolidate the reputation of Italian engineering and create new international avenues for the country's construction firms.
This final phase in his career gave rise to what may be Nervi's most famous work: the papal audience hall in the Vatican (1964-1971), in which Nervi had one last opportunity to work with his own men and equipment. In a context laden with history, he once again assumed his unique role, one that has become anachronistic: architect, builder and supervisor of works all in one, a "master builder" in the best Italian construction tradition.

[7] P.L. Nervi, *Costruire correttamente. Caratteristiche e possibilità delle strutture cementizie armate*, Milan: Hoepli, 1955 (translated in 1956 by Giuseppina and Mario Salvadori under the title *Structures*, published by F.W. Dodge Corporation of New York). In 1965 a second edition of the volume was published in Italy, revised and expanded with information on works built in the past decade.
[8] A volume on Nervi was included in the "The Masters of World Architecture" series, the only Italian in a series of 11 architects from all over the world (when the volume was published, the volumes previously published included Le Corbusier, Wright, Gaudì, Mies Van der Rohe, Aalto). A.L. Huxtable, *Pier Luigi Nervi*, New York: George Braziller Inc., 1960 (also published in Italian, German and Spanish in the same year).
[9] In the 1961-1962 academic year Nervi taught a series of lessons at Harvard University known as the Charles Eliot Norton lectures, published in the volume P.L. Nervi, *Aesthetics and Technology in Building*, Cambridge: Harvard University Press, 1965 (translation by Robert Einaudi). Between May 12 and June 18 1961 a solo show dedicated to Nervi was held at the San Francisco Museum of Art, the catalogue of which was published as P.L. Nervi, *Space and Structural Integrity (May 12 - June 18, 1961)*, San Francisco: San Francisco Museum of Art, 1961. In addition to the RIBA Royal Gold Medal, in 1964 Nervi won the AIA Gold Medal, the top American architecture award.
[10] P.L. Nervi, *Nuove strutture*, Milan: Edizioni di Comunità, 1963 (also published in German and English in the same year).

Chronology

1891 Born in Sondrio on 21 June to Antonio and Luisa Bartoli

1913 Graduates with a civil engineering degree on 28 July from the Scuola di Applicazione in Bologna
Employee of Società Anonima per Costruzioni Cementizie di Attilio Muggia, Hennebique licensee for central Italy

1915 Serves in the Corps of Engineers during the First World War
Files patents for hydrogen-powered engines

1919 Employee of the Florence offices of Società Anonima per Costruzioni Cementizie
Plans and supervises work on Pelota Hall in Florence

1923 Moves to Rome and founds Ing. Nervi & Nebbiosi
Politeama Bruno Banchini in Prato
Plans and supervises work on the bridge over the Cecina in Saline di Volterra

1924 Marries Irene Calosi

1925 Antonio, the first of four children, is born

1926 Teatro Augusteo in Naples

1928 Palazzina a Lungotevere Arnaldo da Brescia, Rome (designed by G. Capponi)

1930 Florence Stadium (covered stands)

1932 Dissolves the company with Nebbiosi and founds Ingg. Nervi & Bartoli with his cousin G. Bartoli
Florence Stadium (completion of stands and spiral staircases)
Plan for circular aircraft hangars
Plan for a rotating building
Plan for a floating hotel (with R. Magnani)

1933 Plan for typical buildings for the 5th Milan Triennial (with C. Valle)
Plan for the Monument to the flag

1934 Plan for a bridge over the Biedano gully, Viterbo

1935 First set of two aircraft hangars, Orvieto
Plan for a 100,000 seat stadium in Rome (with C. Valle)

1936 Underground tanks for a fuel storage facility for the navy (built various tanks of different sizes in different parts of Italy until 1942)

1938 Plan for Solvay silos in Rosignano

1939 Patent no. 377969 for "Structural prefabrication"
Second set of aircraft hangars in Orvieto, Orbetello and Torre del Lago Puccini
Plans for the E42, Rome: Palazzo dell'Acqua e della Luce, exhibition halls A and B (with P.M. Bardi), construction method for monumental arch (designed by A. Libera)

1943 Patent no. 406296 for "Ferrocement" (completed in 1944 by patent no. 429331)
Plans for large ferrocement roofs (train stations, airports)

1945 Ferrocement warehouse in Magliana, Rome
Publishes *Scienza o arte del costruire?*

1946 Plans for prefabricated homes for the reconstruction of Italy
165 ton motorboat Irene
Santa Rita fishing boat

1947 Hall B at Torino Esposizioni
Tourism Pavilion at Fiera di Milano (with G. Oberti), completed in 1953 by an avant-corps
Teaches technology and building techniques at the Faculty of Architecture at La Sapienza University in Rome (until 1962)

1948 Patent no. 445781 for "wave blocks"
Nennele cruising ketch

1949 Patent no. 455678 for "Floor with isostatic ribbing" (with A. Arcangeli)
Swimming pool at Livorno naval academy
"La Tebaide" docks in San Michele di Pagana, Rapallo, Genoa (designed by C. Daneri)
Tobacco workshop in Bologna
Plans for an aircraft hangar in Buenos Aires

1950 Patent no. 465636 for "Tavelloni romboidali": diamond-shaped hollow flat blocks
Hall C at Torino Esposizioni
Salt warehouses, Tortona
Restaurant and trampoline at Kursaal bathing resort (designed by A. Lapadula)
Honorary degree from the Faculty of Architecture of Buenos Aires University (the first of many)
Publishes *El lenguaje arquitectonico*

1951 Gatti wool factory in Rome (with C. Cestelli Guidi)
Design for a bridge over the Reno River, Sasso Marconi, Bologna (with C. Cestelli Guidi)

1952 Unesco offices in Paris (with M. Breuer and B.H. Zehrfuss)
Party room in Chianciano spa (designed by M. Loreti and M. Marchi)
High pressure pipelines made by patented procedure

1953 Design for Sports Hall, Vienna (with A. Nervi)
Design for Lancia factory, Turin

1954 Founds Studio Nervi-Architettura e tecnica edilizia, first with his son Antonio, after 1960 including his other two sons, Mario and Vittorio
Municipal tram deposit, Turin
Tobacco workshop warehouses, Bologna
Structural plan for CNIT, Paris (design by R. Camelot, J. de Mailly, B.H. Zehrfuss)
Plan for central station, Naples (with M. Campanella and G. Vaccaro)

1955 Pirelli skyscraper, Milan (with A. Danusso; design by G. Ponti, A. Fornaroli, A. Rosselli, G. Valtolina, E. Dall'Orto)
Ceilings for Galbani offices, Milan (design by Eu. Soncini, Er. Soncini, G. Pestalozza)
Industrial buildings for Fiat, Turin
Roof for church in the Borgo Panigale district, Bologna (design by G. Vaccaro)
Plan for a bridge over the Tenza River
Plan for Palazzo dello Sport, Florence (with A. Nervi)
Publishes *Costruire correttamente*

1956 Palazzetto dello Sport in Rome (with A. Vitellozzi)
Palazzo dello Sport in Rome (with M. Piacentini)
Flaminio Stadium in Rome (with A. Nervi)
Plan for an exhibition centre, Caracas
Stadium, Taormina (with A. Nervi)

1957 Plan for Leonardo da Vinci International Airport in Fiumicino, Rome (with C. Ligini, U. Luccichenti, A. Nervi, D. Ortensi, G. Vaccaro)

1958 Viaduct in Corso Francia (general urban plan: with V. Cafiero, A. Libera, A. Luccichenti, V. Monaco, L. Moretti)
Plan for New Norcia Cathedral, Australia (with A. Nervi, F. Vacchini, C. Vannoni)

1959	Palazzo del Lavoro for Italia '61, Turin (with A. Nervi and G. Covre) Railway station, Savona (with A. Nervi) Plan for Palazzo del Ghiaccio, Rome (with A. Nervi)
1960	RIBA Royal Gold Medal Cartiera Burgo, Mantua (with G. Covre)
1961	Exhibition of works and plans at the San Francisco Museum of Art Professorship of Poetry at Harvard University: Charles Eliot Norton lectures Bus station, New York Indoor sports field at Dartmouth College, Hanover, New Hampshire Plan for Sports Hall in Kassel, Germany (with A. Nervi) Plan for indoor hippodrome in Richmond, Virginia Plan for Fiera del mare, Genoa (with C. Daneri, A. Nervi) Plan for stands and clubhouse at Liberty Bell Park hippodrome, Philadelphia, Pennsylvania (with A. Nervi)
1962	Stock Exchange Tower in Place Victoria, Montreal, Canada (with L. Moretti and Studio Greenspoon, Freedlander and Dunne) Plan for the Schedeldoekshaven complex, the Hague
1963	Cassa di Risparmio bank, Venice (with A. Scattolin) Ponte Risorgimento, Verona Plan for church in the ANIC district, Ravenna (with A. Nervi) Publishes *Nuove strutture*
1964	AIA Gold Medal Audience hall in the Vatican Australia Tower, Sydney, Australia (design by H. Seidler) Plan for the Fermi Memorial, Chicago
1965	Plan for expansion of Portsmouth Cathedral (with Studio Seely & Paget) Publishes *Aesthetics and Technology in Building*
1966	Cromodora building, Venaria Reale, Turin BIT offices, Geneva, Switzerland (with E. Beaudoin and A. Camenzind) St. Mary's Cathedral, San Francisco (with P. Belluschi and Studio McSweeney, Ryan & Lee) Sports Hall, Norfolk, Virginia (with Studio Williams & Tazewell) Plan for Pitt Rivers Museum, Oxford (with Powell & Moya) Plan for cultural centre in Tripoli, Libya Plan for Sports Hall, Vicenza (with A. Nervi, P. Moltauro)
1967	Arena at Dartmouth College, Hanover, New Hampshire (with A. Nervi) Motta service station in Limena, Padua (with M. Bega, A. Nervi) Plan for Ruhr-Universität auditorium, Bochum, Germany (with Hentrich, Petschnigg & Partner)
1968	Banca d'Italia security paper printing shop, Rome (with A. Nervi) Plan for sports centre in Kuwait City, Kuwait
1969	Italian embassy, Brasilia, Brazil (with A. Nervi) Plan for bridge over the Strait of Messina (with A. Nervi) Plan for Palazzo dello Sport, Milan (with A. Nervi)
1970	Good Hope Centre, Cape Town, South Africa (with A. Nervi)
1979	Dies in Rome on January 9 (on June 22 his eldest son Antonio also dies, and shortly after this Studio Nervi closes)

Works

G. Berta Municipal Stadium

Florence, Italy, 1930-1933

View of the stadium's exterior

Florence stadium is the first of Pier Luigi Nervi's major projects, which met with the critics' approval in Italy and abroad. The elegant lines of the cantilever roof over the stands and the dynamic weave of the access stairways became a symbol of the figurative potential of reinforced concrete, at that time a new material still to be explored, for his generation of architects. Nervi, who dominated the material by virtue of his twenty years of experience building large-scale structures, makes the most of its capacity for resistance here, reducing sections to a minimum and directing the forces in play along skilfully optimised paths. The result is surprising. The cantilever roof seems to have been shaped by the wind, like a bird's wing. Supported by 24 weight-bearing shelves, it is however kept in perfect balance not by the thrust of the air but by the action of the strut, which cuts the overhang by half and is admirably integrated into the building's aerodynamic profile, and by the stabilising counterweight of the body of the stands. Similarly, the ramp of the stairway protrudes like a shelf out of a spiral-shaped girder, which crosses a symmetrical girder halfway along. This not only gives the overall design

The soccer field seen from the stands

a perfect balance of almost classical proportions, but also plays a very important static role, reducing the twisting action generated by the ramp in the main spiral-shaped girder.
When presenting the project, the engineer did not hide the fact that he could not explain the functioning of the staircase through mathematical calculation. Only the client's faith in his intuition and very strict load tests conducted during testing permitted creation of this minor masterpiece.
The stadium, originally named "Giovanni Berta" and now named after Artemio Franchi, built by the City in the former Campo di Marte area, has always hosted the Fiorentina football team's home games. It was built in two stages: first the stands sheltered by the cantilever roof, designed in March 1930 and completed in November 1931, then the uncovered stands with the three spiral staircases and the symbolic Marathon tower, completed in 1932. The stadium was adapted for the 1990 Football World Cup, changing its image (adding two new portions of cantilever roof, made of steel, at either side of the original roof, which hid its beautiful profile).

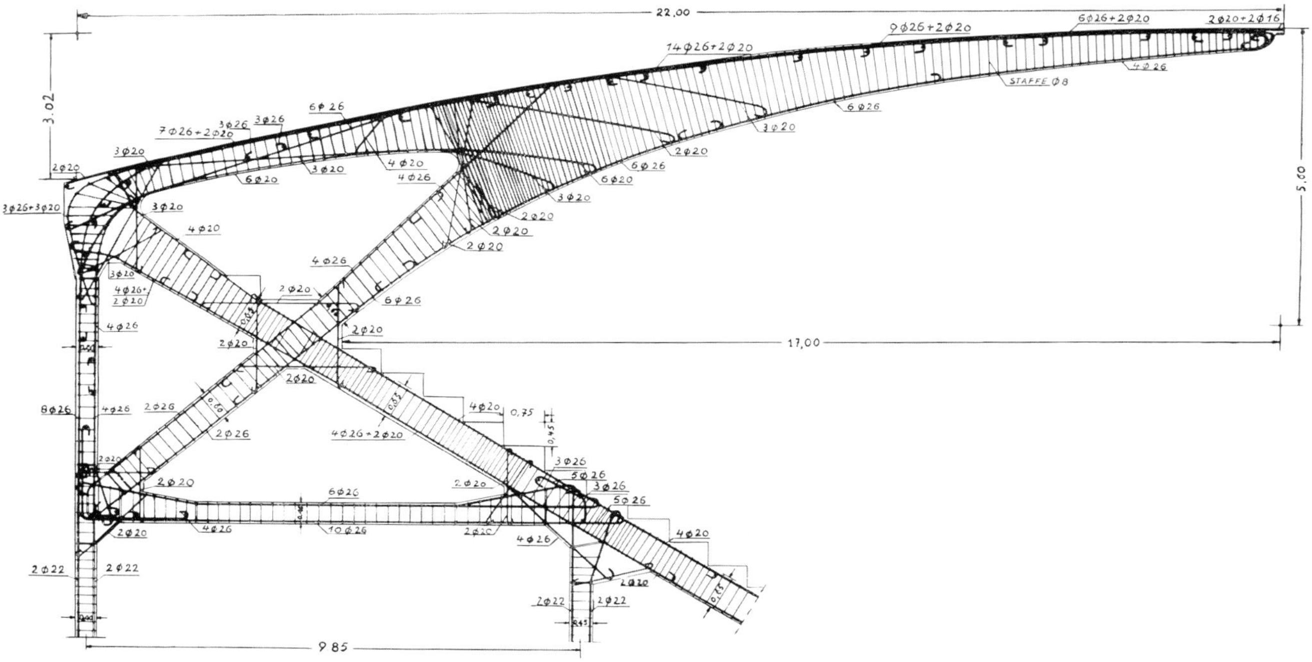

above
Executive drawing
for the cantilever roof

side
Construction
of the cantilever roof

opposite page
View of the staircase

POPOLARI
L.4
POPOLARI
L.4

Geodetic Aircraft Hangars

Orvieto airport, Castel Viscardo, Italy, 1935-1938 (first series); 1939-1942 (second series)

First series, model by Danusso

Four aircraft hangars were designed by Nervi and built by his construction firm, Nervi & Bartoli, on the Alfina plateau, where Orvieto Airport was opened in 1938, closed after the war. These gigantic structures, which could cover the surface of a football field and were 12 to 20 metres high, were intended to protect the fleet from bombs. Conceived as big pavilion-like grid vaults, formed by two sets of identical arches meeting at right angles, they were raised above the ground by inclined pylons. Airplanes entered the hangars through either one of the long sides, where colossal sliding doors opened to a width of over fifty metres. Once completed, they would have looked from above like robust carapaces of some extinct animal species. The inventiveness of their construction, creating a weave in the ribbing in a manner akin to embroidery, is an interesting aspect of these projects. Built in two series, though almost identical on the outside, the two versions of the aircraft hangar are actually very different. The evolution between the two versions marked Nervi's transition from ordinary construction to "structural prefabrication." The first two hangars, designed on the occasion of a competition held by the Royal Air Force in 1935, were built by the usual

reinforced concrete technique; that is, by preparing wooden formworks, which are very complicated and expensive in view of the structure of the roof, arranging the structure and casting them on site. But in the second pair of identical hangars, built in 1940 and 1942 near the Orbetello and Torre del Lago Puccini air harbours, the structure of the arches is broken down into small grid-like fragments made of reinforced concrete cast on the ground, in forms assembled using simple wooden boards, then lifted to rest on a light metal scaffold and linked together by casting in position. This operation of breaking them down and putting them back together, which the engineer patented as his own invention, turned out to be exceptionally economical and quick, and became the basis of the "Nervi method" after the war. Both versions of the hangars are too complicated to be scaled using ordinary calculations, and so Nervi began a process of experimental research based on small-scale celluloid models, which allowed him to simulate and predict the real structure's behaviour. All the hangars in the two series were destroyed by Allied bombs or by retreating Nazi forces during the Second World War.

Second series, construction site

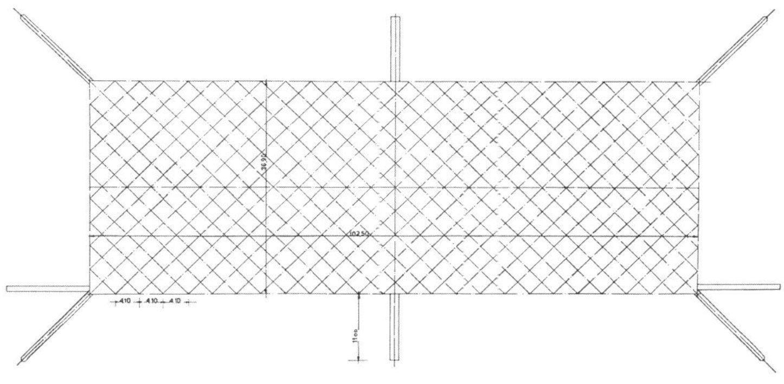

above
Interior of an aircraft hangar in the first series

below
Plan for an aircraft hangar in the second series

opposite page
First series, exterior with detail of door

Hall B

Torino Esposizioni complex, Turin, Italy, 1947-1948

The construction site

This exhibition space, opened in September 1948 during the 23rd Salone dell'Automobile (Automobile Expo), was enthusiastically received by critics from all over the world, who instantly recognised as a masterpiece. It was built in just ten months, immediately after the end of the war, despite a myriad of organisational and economic difficulties. This is in part thanks to the first large-scale application of the "Nervi method" which adopted the engineer's two major inventions: a new material, ferrocement, and a revolutionary technique, "structural prefabrication."

The hall is set up like a contemporary basilica: a vaulted central nave with aisles at either side, lit up entirely from above, closed at the end by a semi-circular apse covered with a ribbed half-dome. Particularly striking, the vault consists in waves of ferrocement set side by side, only a few centimetres thick (an average of three), cross connected by diaphragms and emptied out at the sides to allow the filtering of light. These thin waves are resistant "by form," that is, by effect of their particular shape. Every three waves, a fan collects and joins forces, transmitting them to an inclined pylon that widens toward the ground and in the foundations. To build the big arches, Nervi

View of the exhibition space

invented a special system which he promptly patented. He broke the waves down into small blocks (about four metres long) made on the ground by spreading cement over a fine metal mesh of appropriate shape. Once they had hardened, the blocks were then raised, assembled on scaffolding and made monolithic by casting in position. In this way a roof more than 90 metres wide was assembled, block after block, at minimal cost and in record time. The semi-circular apse, on the other hand, was created by assembling pieces of another kind, known as *tavelloni romboidali* or diamond-shaped flat hollow blocks (which Nervi also patented). These small fragments are created when the half-dome is broken down as best as possible, on the ground, put back together like pieces of a puzzle, and then cast-joined after being positioned. In 1952, this particular construction technique made it possible to amplify the vault in an unusual manner. New waves, identical to the original ones, were added, transforming the space from a square to a rectangle. The building was adapted to host ice hockey games during the Turin Winter Olympics in 2006 but has now been completely restored and returned to its original use as an exhibition hall.

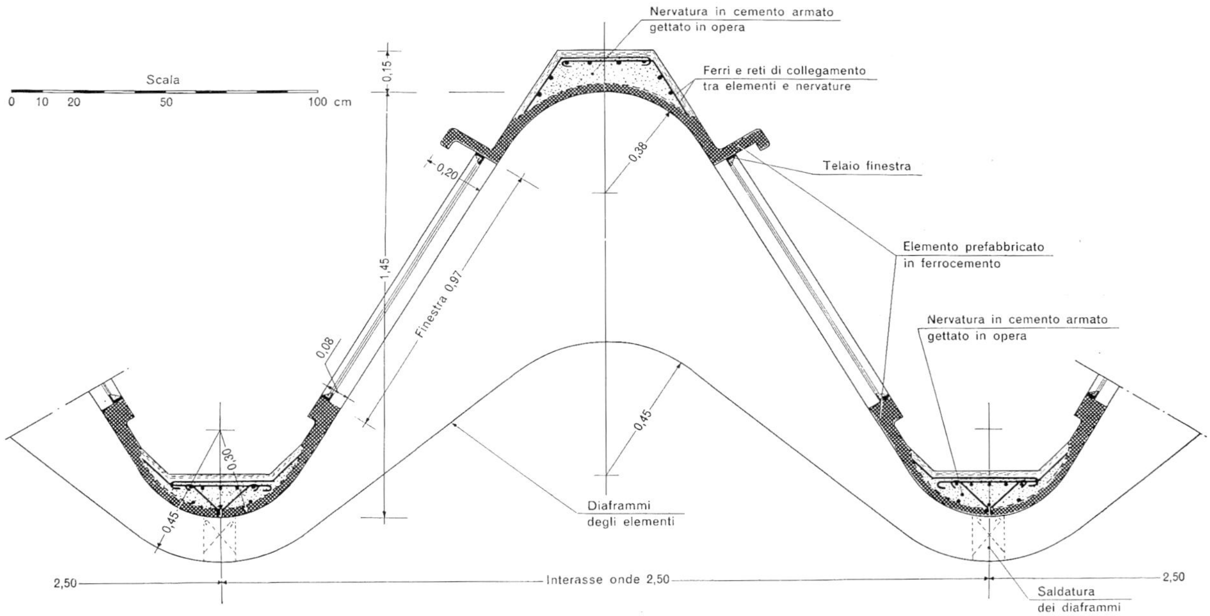
Scala
0 10 20 50 100 cm
Nervatura in cemento armato gettato in opera
Ferri e reti di collegamento tra elementi e nervature
Telaio finestra
Elemento prefabbricato in ferrocemento
Nervatura in cemento armato gettato in opera
Diaframmi degli elementi
Saldatura dei diaframmi
Interasse onde 2,50
Finestra 0,97
0,15
0,38
0,20
1,45
0,08
0,45
0,30
2,50

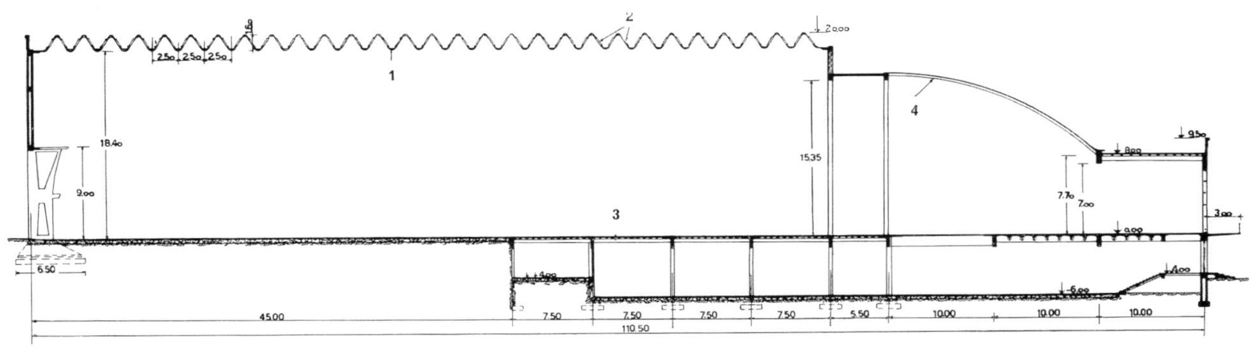
1
2
3
4
18.40
15.35
45.00
110.50
7.50
5.50
10.00

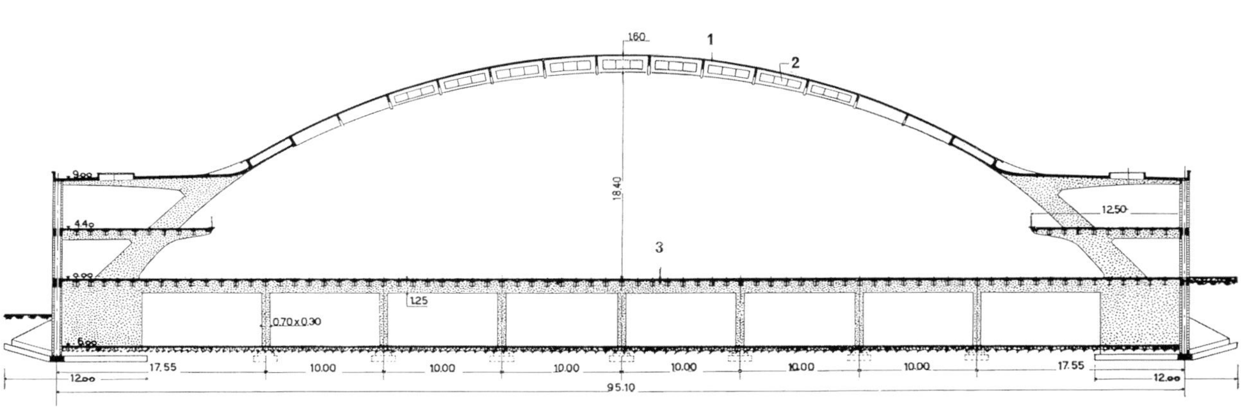
1
2
3
18.40
12.50
0.70x0.30
1.25
17.55
10.00
12.00
95.10

View of the ferrocement vault

opposite page
From above, executive drawing of the wave and longitudinal and cross sections

Gatti Wool Factory

Rome, Italy, 1951

Aerial view of the construction site

Designed by Carlo Cestelli Guidi, the portion of the industrial edifice that is the subject of this commentary involves solely the basement warehouse. Here, the application of Nervi's inventions produces unique architectural results. This small room, preserved due to its inconvenient position, is one of the first applications of the famous isostatic ribbed ceiling method.

The lovely design produced by causing the ribbing to branch out in a "mushroom-like" formation from the pillars is not, as might seem, intended to serve a decorative function; rather, the embroidered pattern is a natural result of the isostatic bending lines of a slab under a load. Nervi arranged the material along those lines where it would best be able to collaborate in resistance. By observing the material's natural behaviour, and adapting his plan to it, he was able to achieve the utmost economical solution possible.

This approach should not come as a surprising revelation given that Nervi had always demonstrated great curiosity in the harmony and continuity in the manner in which stress is distributed in bodies. With the

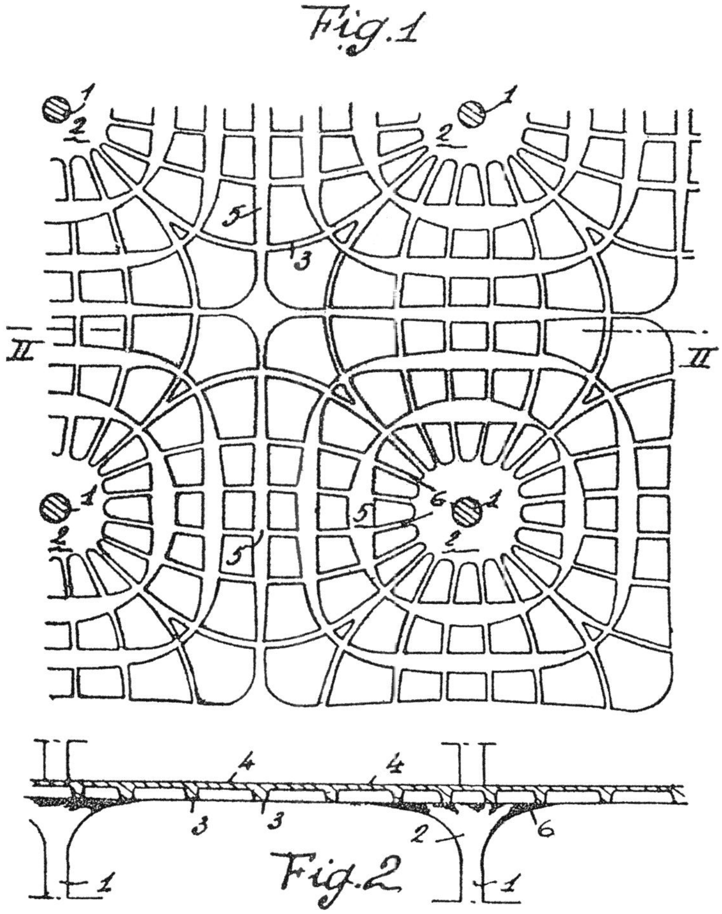

invention of the isostatic ribbed slab, patented in 1949, he managed to make this joyful natural equilibrium perceptible even to the layman.
Imitation of natural force lines is, however, rendered feasible and economical only by using the "Nervi method." It would have been too costly to reproduce the curved geometries of the reinforced concrete slab with ordinary wooden formworks thus Nervi prepared a form as big as an entire field between the pillars, putting together bottomless hollow boxes with a soft profile that adapts to the design of the isostatic lines, created thanks to the mouldable quality of ferrocement. This square form was then assembled on a trolley, which could be moved on wheels and re-used to contain the reinforced concrete cast for all the squares. At the end of the job, the repetition of identical fields generated a capricious arabesque dictated by the wisdom of nature.
The warehouse was believed to have been destroyed but in actual fact still exists, improperly used as a workshop and garage for automobiles.

Patent for flooring with isostatic ribs

Panoramic view of the basement warehouse and detail

Detail of prefabricated ferrocement formworks

side
Partial plan

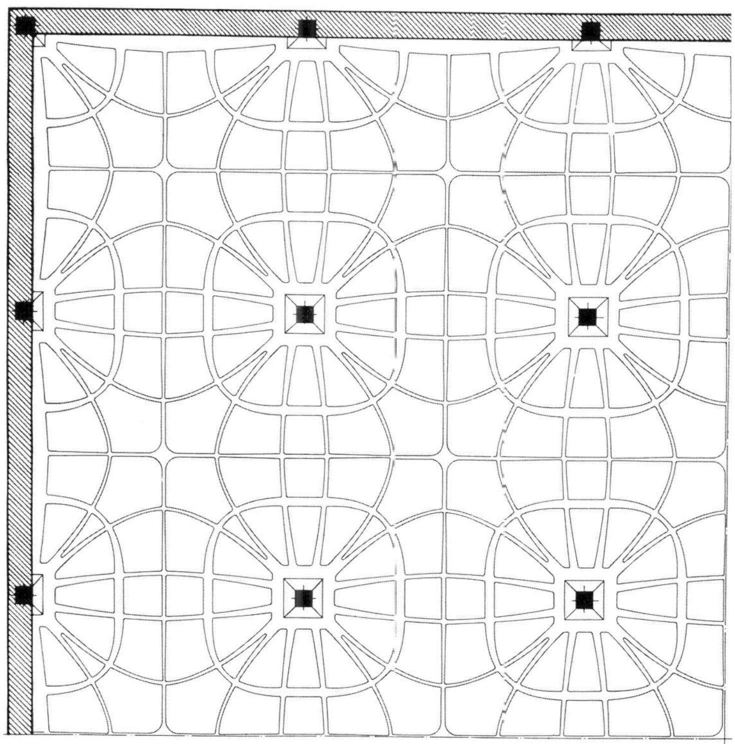

Unesco Offices

Paris, France, 1952-1958

Exterior with row of giant pillars

Just after the war Unesco, the United Nations' cultural and scientific agency, founded in November 1945, decided to build its headquarters in Paris and appointed a prestigious commission to choose its architects. In July 1952 five world-renowned architects (Lucio Costa, Le Corbusier, Walter Gropius, Sven Markelius, Ernesto N. Rogers), representing different countries, selected a team of three architects to design the new headquarters on the basis of the latter's portfolios: Marcel Breuer of the US, Bernard H. Zehrfuss of France and Pier Luigi Nervi of Italy. This was the first concrete international acknowledgement of Nervi's talent.

In motivating their decision, the judges identified him as one of the world's most brilliant engineers. The complex includes a seven-storey office building shaped like a three-pointed star, raised on pilotis, with a cubic volume set up to host delegations, and

a conference room, located in a separate area, nick-named "the accordion."
This is the building in which Nervi's style is most evident. The static solution adopted determines the whole's entire architectural image, dominated by the characteristic folding of the roof and the walls, ensuring resistance "by form," just as a thin piece of paper becomes stronger if folded repeatedly in "accordion folds."
The corrugated surface of the roof is generated by the juxtaposition of large longitudinal girders with a broken axis, marked by a V-shaped section, set into the walls at either end and made to rest in an asymmetrical position inside the space on a row of pillars of complex shape.
The waves vary in height along the axis of development on the basis of differing loads. A compression-resistant slab resistant supports the folded section, running sinuously along, intersecting the V in variable positions to assist the moment diagram. The pillars also change shape as they rise: circular at the base, they are transformed into rectangles at the top, and their surface area is determined by the line uniting homologous points on the two sections. Like the roof, the walls are also given greater resistance by their repeated folds.
With its exposed concrete surface, the hall has an austere, simple appearance of imposing architectural expressiveness.

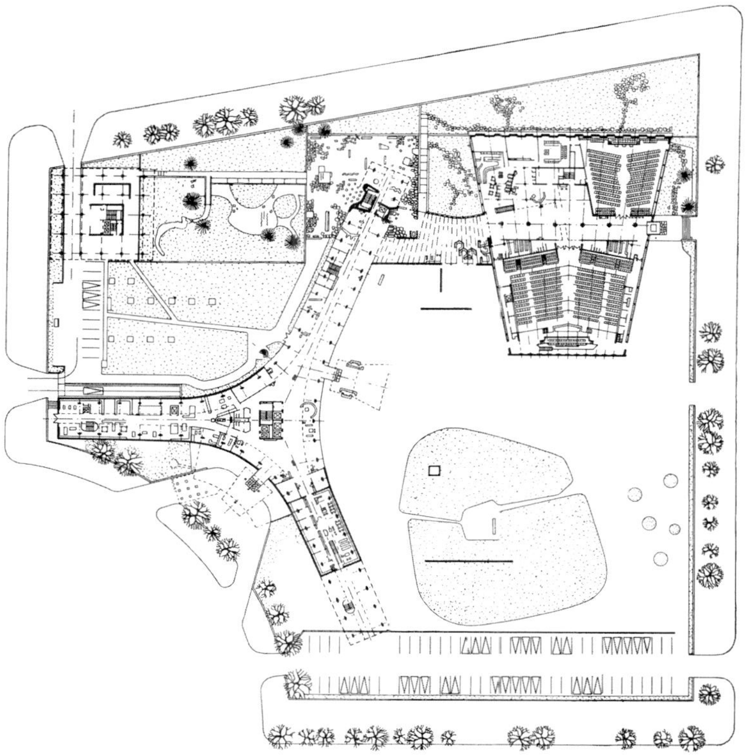

Plan of the complex

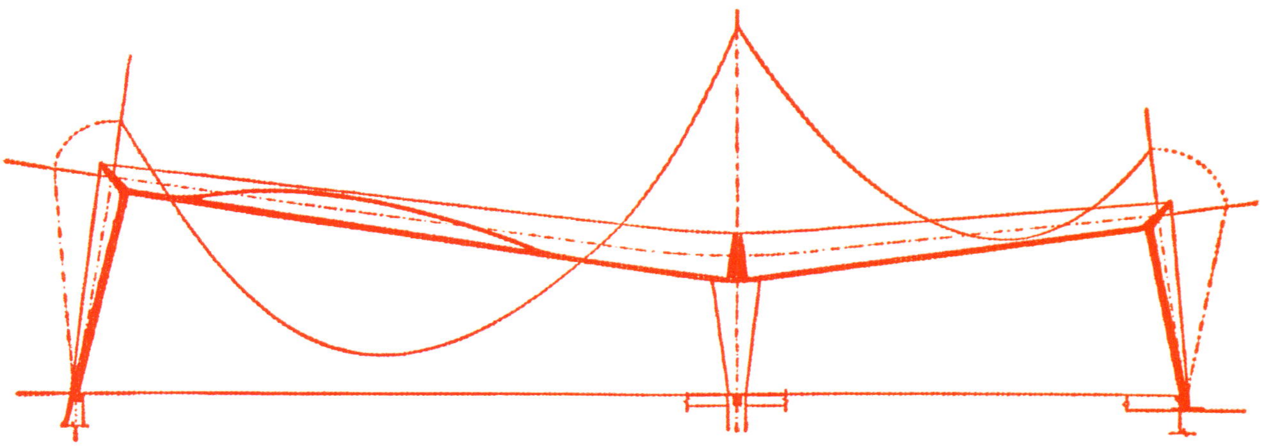

above
View of the building
and, below, static diagram
of the roof on the hall

above
Panoramic view
of the complex

side
Model

Pirelli Skyscraper

Milan, Italy, 1955-1960

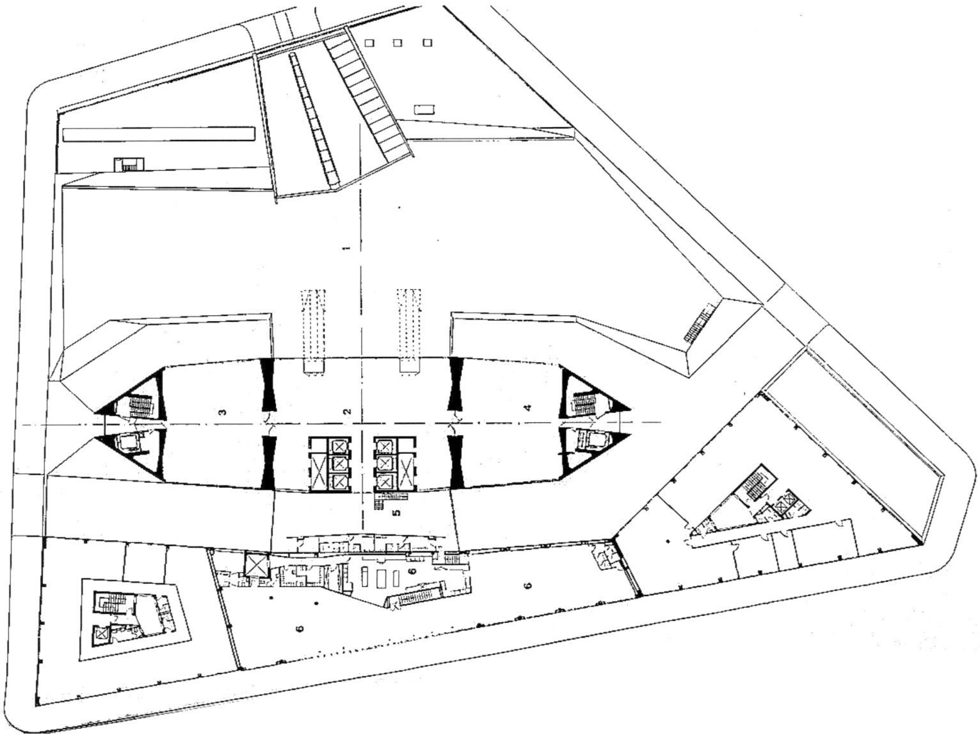

Plan of the ground floor

One of the world's tallest reinforced concrete buildings (127 metres), the skyscraper is a symbol of Milan. The building's architectural design is by Gio Ponti, leader of a team of architects and engineers who had already worked with him in the studio; however, Nervi is the mastermind of the structural solution. He was assisted in his endeavours by Arturo Danusso, one of Italy's most important theoreticians and experimenters in 20th century construction science. The decision to use reinforced concrete rather than steel, a material that would certainly have been preferred internationally, was ordained by its cost-effectiveness, in terms of design and construction, an important consideration given Italy's productive ad corporate reality at that time.

Nervi's design deviates from common models for tall buildings. His project was centred on the notion that the skyscraper should act as an elastic shelf, set into the ground, capable of oscillating in the wind. To the contrary, Nervi imagined a "gravity" scheme for his tower similar to those employed for masonry dams. He widened the foundation and stabilised the load-bearing vertical elements by giving them sufficient size and weight to

ensure equilibrium at the base. He therefore decided to concentrate the resistant section in two pairs of central dividing walls, with a butterfly shape, and two hollow triangular elements at either end. Ceiling and floor slabs weave in parallel to the façades while the central portion boasts an impressive 24-metre span. The weight-bearing pylons are perfectly visible along the building's façades, as the structure is level with the glass and interrupts its continuity.
To confirm Nervi's static intuitions, Danusso – who had contributed to the engineer's static experiments right from the days of the aircraft hangars – made a large test model in his laboratory, measuring almost 9 metres in height, which he used to simulate the tower's behaviour under horizontal forces.
Bought in 1978 as office space for the Region of Lombardy, the building was recently subjected to an accurate philological restoration, made necessary when a small plane crashed into the twenty-sixth floor and killed three people on April 18, 2002. The restoration project primarily involved the curtain-wall on the façade, as the structure was not damaged except at the point of impact.

left
Model for static tests in the Ismes laboratory in Bergamo

right
Model of the structure

left
Axonometric cross section, drawing by G. Capurso

right
Diagram of the structure

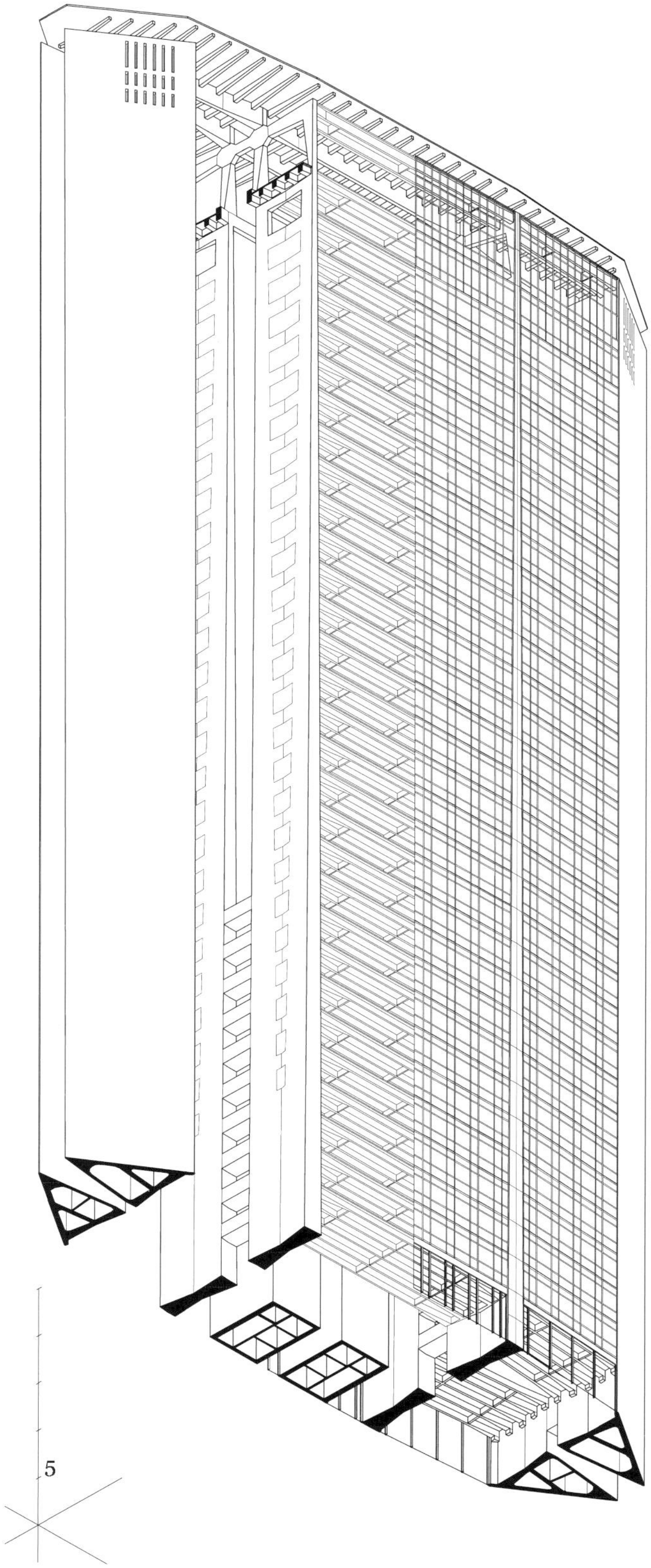

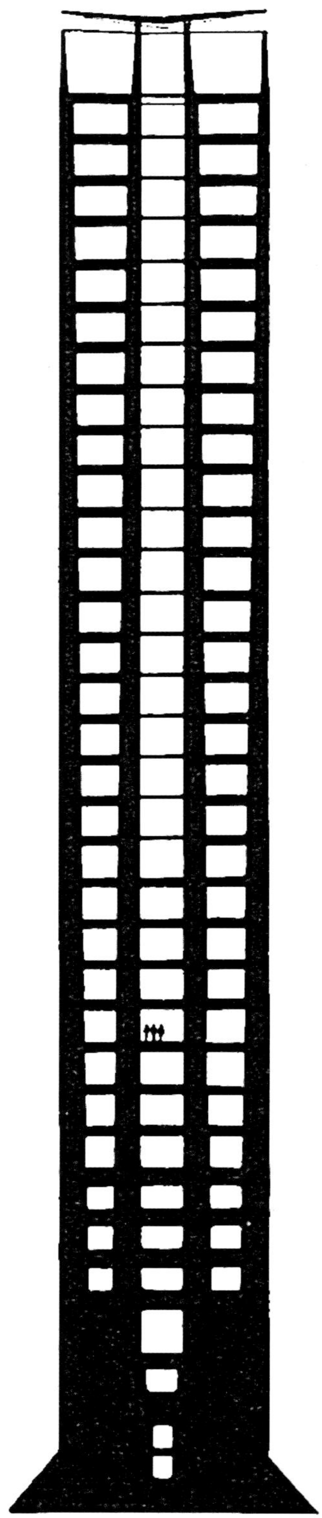

View of the building

Palazzetto dello Sport
Rome, Italy, 1956-1957

Construction site

Built for the 1960 Rome Olympics, the Palazzetto dello Sport is one of Nervi's most famous constructions. It looks like a perfectly inflated crown, ready to take off if not for the fact that it is tightly anchored to the ground by 36 radial inclined trestles, between whose diverging antennas the festooned edge sways. The unique shape of the dome, perfectly smooth on the outside, is all the more particular on the inside, where a weave of cross ribbing creates a series of big diamonds in an evocative optic game. In effect, the construction is a milestone in Nervi's career. It is the most mature expression of his static, constructive and architectural experimentation, finally sealing recognition of his original construction method. His project was inspired by his own principal inventions: structural prefabrication and ferrocement. The dome is, in fact, broken down into little "rhomboid hollow flat blocks," prefabricated on the ground at the construction site by simply spreading conglomerate over a shape prepared with steel mesh to a thickness of 3 centimetres. The hollow flat blocks, which are particularly economical, lightweight and easy for workers to carry, are positioned on a metal scaffold.

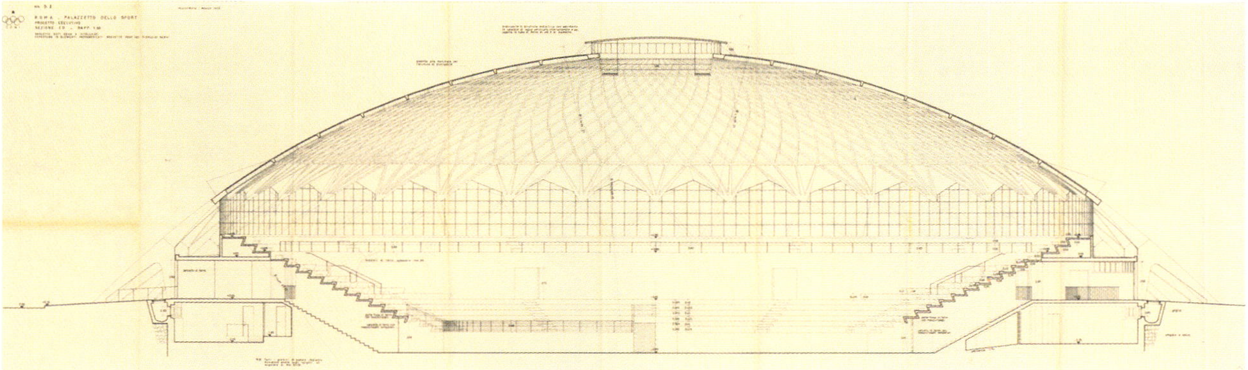

above
Cross section

side
Aerial view

Since they are rimmed at the edges, they may be set together to form channels which, when appropriately reinforced, constitute the formworks for casting the cement in position. Upon completion, the structure acts and looks like a monolithic dome, and there is nothing to suggest the minute breakdown that actually underlies the construction process. The technique made it possible to build the entire building in only 14 months. While conventional techniques were used to build the trestles around the outside, all the hollow flat blocks were made together, optimising efficiency at the site. A team effort, the project was completed thanks to the collaboration of Annibale Vitellozzi, of the technical office of COR, the public organisation specially founded to build the facilities for the Olympics. In the gap of time – years – between the commissioning of the work and the inauguration of the Games, Nervi and his company also designed and built three more famous projects: the Palazzo dello Sport in the Eur district, spanned by a 100 metre dome; Flaminio Stadium, in collaboration with his son Antonio, with its characteristic cantilever roof; and the Corso Francia viaduct serving the Olympic Village.

Air One

Interior of the Palazzetto

Palazzo del Lavoro
Turin, Italy, 1959-1961

To celebrate the centennial of the unification of Italy, Turin hosted a world exposition between May and October of 1961. A large area next to the Po River became the construction site of new buildings, intended to host events and exhibitions, serviced by futuristic transportation systems. Nervi won a tender in July 1959 for the design and construction of the building that was to host the most important exhibition, centred on the theme "Man at Wor." His projected, selected among many put forth by several prestigious groups of Italian architects and engineers, was ideated in tandem with his son, Antonio, who had by then been working with his father for several years. Gino Covre, Italy's most authoritative structurist with regard to metal constructions was also an important collaborator.

This colossal project (25,000 sq.m) was to be completed with an exceptionally tight schedule: red tape had delayed the start of construction, so that work on the foundations could not begin until February 1960, when only twelve months were left to complete the building and set up the exhibition in time for its opening. Nervi resolved this complex problem by breaking

The building from the outside

page 64
From the top, detail of the roof, mushroom-shaped pillar during construction and advertising poster for the Italia '61 exposition

page 65
Interior with exhibition stands

down the volume into a parallelepiped prism with a square base, in 16 separate but identical squares, each formed of a pilaster of reinforced concrete from the top of which steel brackets radiated outward. The speed of construction was impressive. As the big pilasters were being built on site, the roof girders were being made in the workshop, for subsequent rapid assembly one after the other. Concurrently, a raised gallery was being built around the perimeter of the prism, entirely independent from it in structural terms, using the isostatic ribbed slab technique. Once the pilasters and the outer rays had been completed, it was possible to start erecting the curtain-wall of the façade, screened by dense sunshades. These gigantic "mushroom-shaped" elements were visually impacting and skilfully employed by Gio Ponti, artistic director of the exhibition, who left them all fully visible, drawing attention to their essential, almost graphic lines with his installation.
Though the critics called it a "prodigy of architecture," the building was never again used for a suitable unitary person following Italia '61.

Italia 61
Il settore italiano dell'EIL
Un secolo di progresso documentato in sintesi

1961
1861

Burgo Paper Mill

Mantua, Italy, 1960-1964

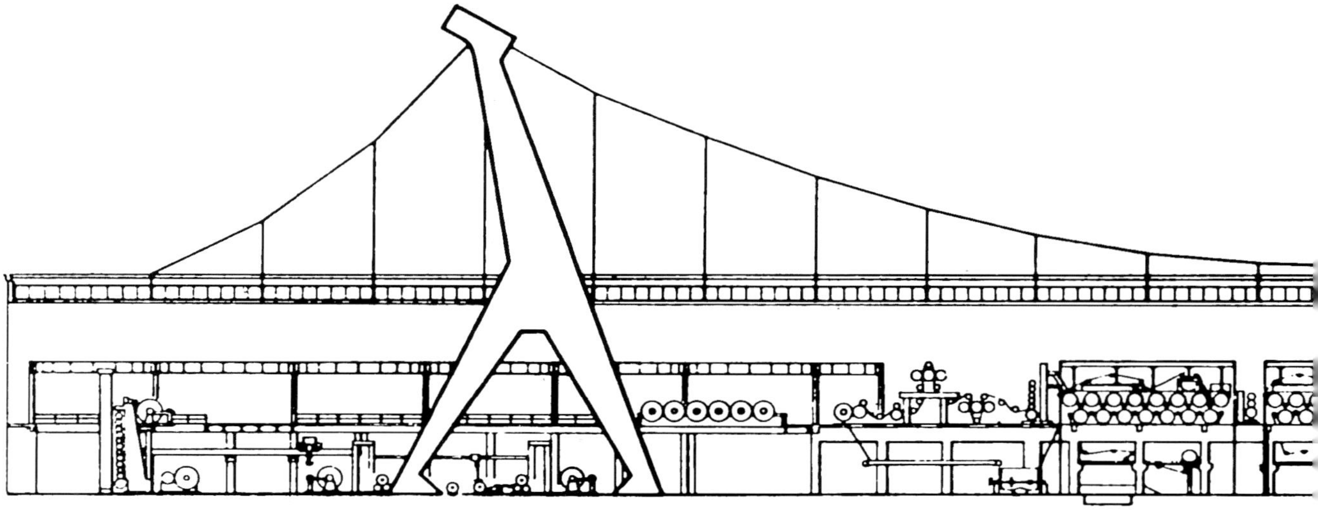

Longitudinal section

page 68
Detail of one of the uprights

page 69
above
The construction site
below
Panoramic view showing the elongated glass structure of the edifice between two large uprights

The paper mill dominates the rolling hills of Mantua, its unique outline resembling a suspension bridge. Nervi, who had never had the opportunity to build a wide span bridge (the Corso Francia viaduct in Rome has spans of only 16 metres; the bridge over the Adige in Verona, which he designed a few years later, has a free central span of 62 metres), elected to work with an industrial building, experimenting a solution normally used only for transportation infrastructures. His original and unusual choice met the strict requisites imposed by the commissioner, Burgo. The structure needed to shelter a huge machine specially built for continuous paper production (more than 100 metres long, it was one of Europe's most innovative and advanced paper machines). Further, the company intended to purchase a second machine to run alongside the first one in the near future. Nervi thus had to create an edifice that could be easily duplicated that would permit access to the machine and its possible future twin from the side. As he could not use an ordinary framed

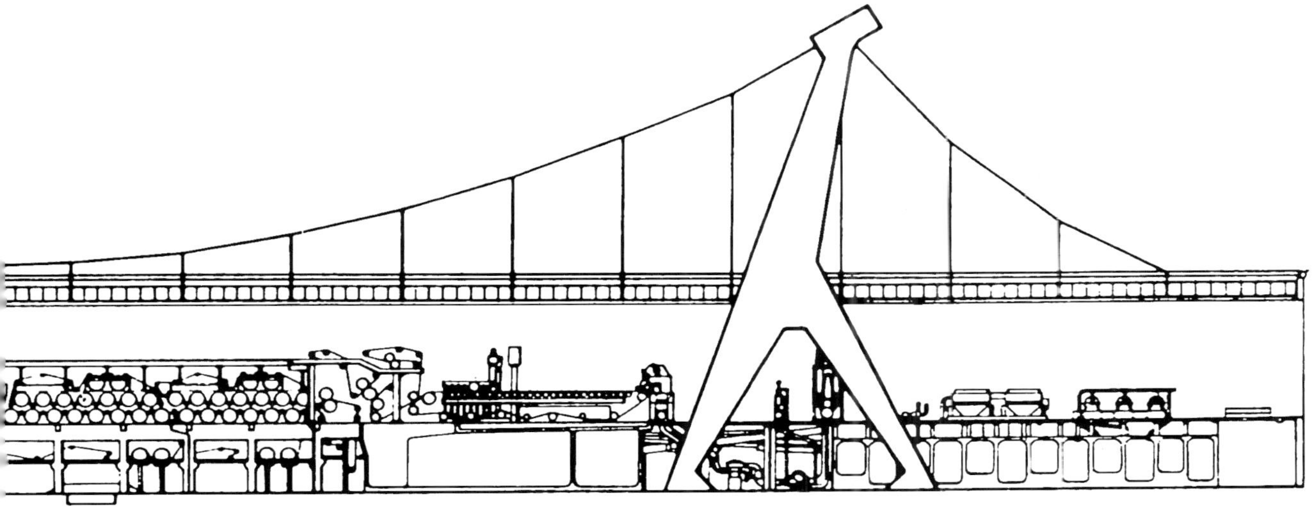

structure, he decided to suspend the roof from two big portals located 164 metres apart. Situated between the pillars of the portals, the long, narrow glass box of the paper mill stands like a structure along a motorway. Masterfully designed to offer the best possible response to the stresses at work, the pillars appear like imposing anthropomorphic forms, akin to players in a tug-of-war game.
The suspension chains hanging from the top of the pillars are composed of jointed flat metal bars, reminiscent of the first 19th century suspension bridges (before the use of iron cables woven in strands). Positioned on the joints along the chains, vertical suspension wires support the surface of the steel roof, designed as a lightweight, easy to assemble grid (also typical of bridge structures). In developing the steel structures, Nervi turned for assistance to Gino Covre, with whom he had shared the success of the Palazzo del Lavoro in Turin. The building is still perfectly functional today, though it was decided almost immediately that its size would not be doubled.

Bus Station

New York, Usa, 1961-1962

The construction site

This is Nervi's first "American" project. Located in the heart of Manhattan, it stands at the end of one of the city's most famous suspension bridges, the 1931 George Washington Bridge, which Le Corbusier had called the world's most beautiful bridge. Following this success, Nervi was then commissioned many more American projects (from the San Francisco Cathedral project in 1964-1970 to the Norfolk Sports Hall in 1971 and sports facilities at Dartmouth College in Hanover in 1962-1975), but this work is definitely of decisive importance for the awarding of the 1964 AIA Gold Medal, the most prestigious American architecture award (in 2008 the prize was awarded to an Italian architect for the second time: Renzo Piano). The Port of New York Authority awarded the bus station project to Nervi, but was later criticised for having weakened the power of this severe, brutal project with affected interior décor and additions in poor taste (the level on which the bus stops are located is more faithful to the original design).
In homage to the nearby steel bridge with its grid pylons, Nervi chose to adopt a triangular weave to resolve the roof and outside walls of

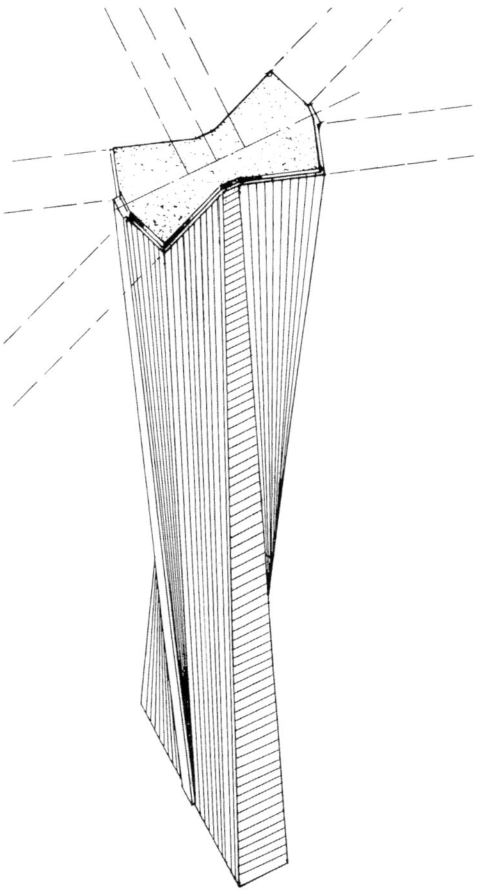

the station, interpreting it with bare reinforced concrete. Seen from above, the imposing sheds on the roof resemble seven oversized butterfly wings, raised just above the central spine as if ready to take flight. As in all his international projects, Nervi was not himself the builder, and so the economical, rational construction system he had perfected over the course of a long career was systematically overturned by local building companies. Since the size of the hollow flat blocks forming the roof are too large, so much so that workers' could not possibly lifting them, the builders had to give up on structural prefabrication. The material used is no longer thin, lightweight ferrocement, but an ordinary reinforced concrete slab. In short, the "Nervi method" is only a memory, evoked by the figures impressed on the surface.

The pillars – the only part made as specified by Nervi – have a very unusual shape: their section is transformed as they rise, twisting them in a motion that seems impossible for cement (but is in actual fact easy to obtain if a line is made in the surface and formworks are made out of ordinary boards).

From left, drawing and view of the pillar

page 72
above
Drawings of the gables on the roof
below
Model

page 73
Aerial view of the complex

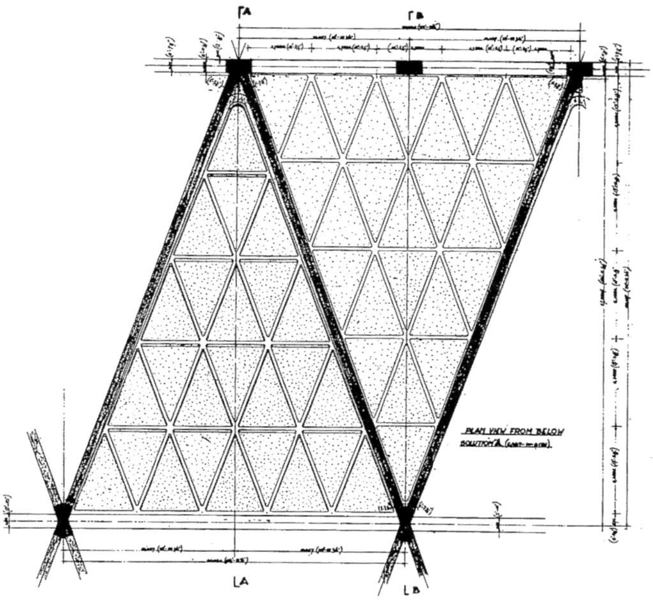
PLAN VIEW FROM BELOW

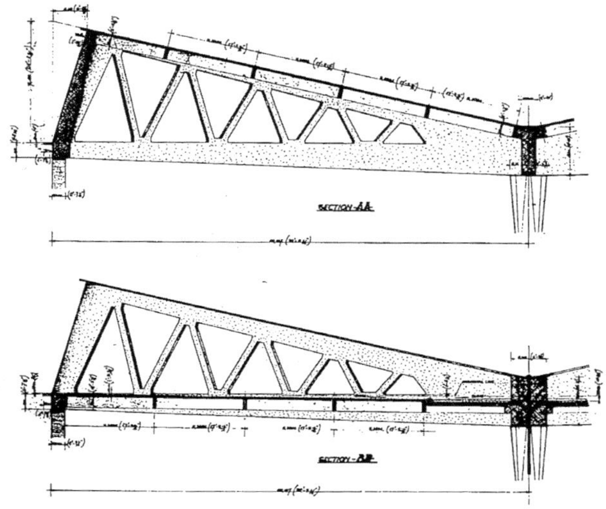
SECTION-AA
SECTION-BB

Audience Hall

Vatican City, 1964-1971

Plan of the hall

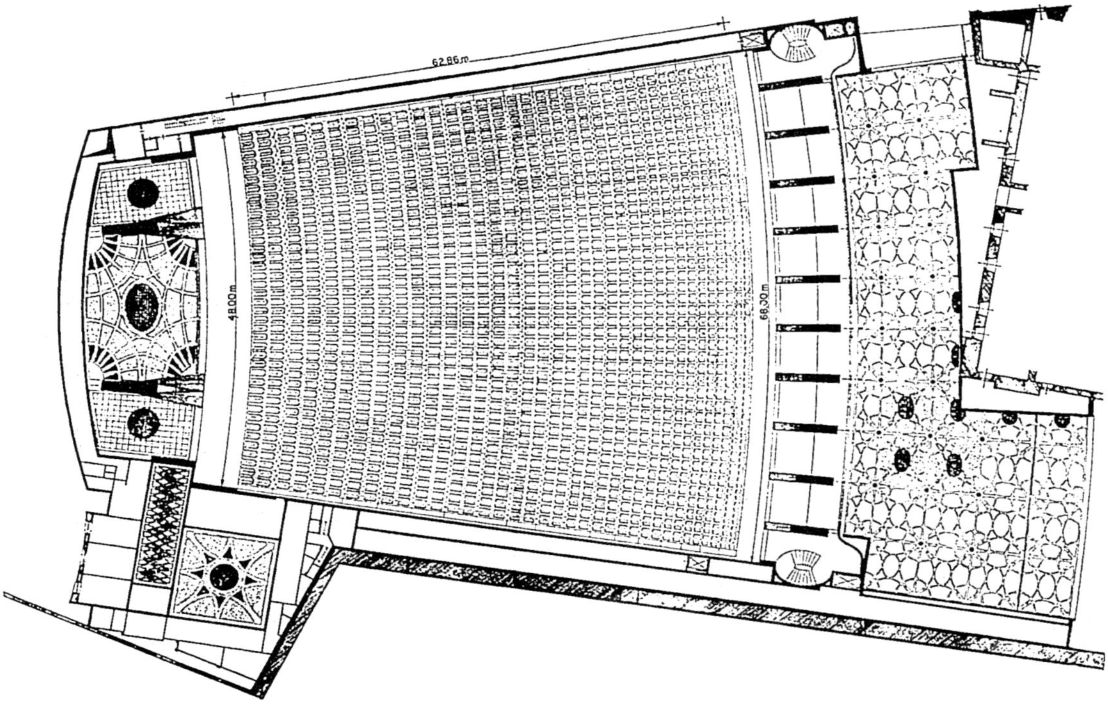

Commonly referred to as the Nervi Hall, although it is officially named after Pope Paul VI, this project is the most difficult that Nervi undertook at the end of his career. He was eighty years old when the hall was inaugurated. When blessing the hall, Paul VI recalled that he had encouraged Nervi to be bold, "knowing that he had the genius and virtue for such enterprises," when, in 1964, he assigned him the difficult task of building project that was not to stand "paltry and banal" in the shadow of St. Peter's basilica. This was a unique project; not a church, not an auditorium, but the place where the Pope held his audiences, a sort of modern Sistine Chapel, a completely new sort of space intended for the faithful in the wake of the opening up of the Catholic church at Vatican II. In honour of this occasion, Nervi took up his most brilliant inventions again, improved them one more time and joined them in a grandiose, spectacular project, which is extraordinarily effective despite its simplicity and essentiality. Flanking the Vatican, the lot made available to him was squeezed in between other buildings and was characterised by an elongated trapezoidal form. The interior spaces, the heart of the design, are covered by a big vault that also fulfils the task of directing the

Interior during construction

attention of the faithful toward the papal throne. The vault is in fact corrugated by an interminable sequence of waves which, as they adapt to the trapezoidal shape of the floor plan, are concentrated toward the stage, coming closer together and higher and then growing farer apart, flatter and wider toward the back of the room. This creates a dynamic tension apparently generated by an ideal fire located to the right of the throne. This dramatic set-up is reinforced by two isolated, large and specially shaped cyclopic pilasters positioned at either side of the stage. These gather the thrust of all the waves, corresponding to an order of smaller, more numerous pilasters at the end of the hall. This particular wave construction was created by refining the tried "Nervi method," consisting of structural prefabrication (the waves are prefabricated, broken down into half-blocks) and ferrocement, the latter masterfully polished in this project. Every element in the structure is in fact made of white cement, blended with special inert matter containing fragments of Apuan marble. All the surfaces are left exposed and no finishing material is used, ensuring that cement, traditionally considered a poor, sad material, is here given the same worth as the precious stones employed in the nearby basilica.

Panoramic view of the hall

below
Longitudinal
and cross sections

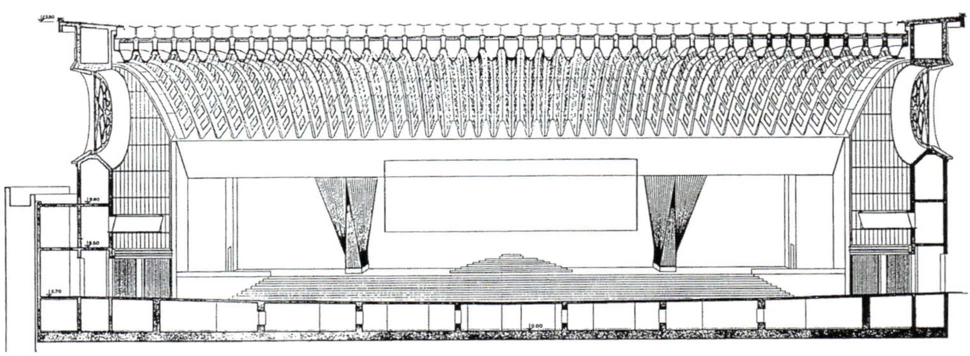

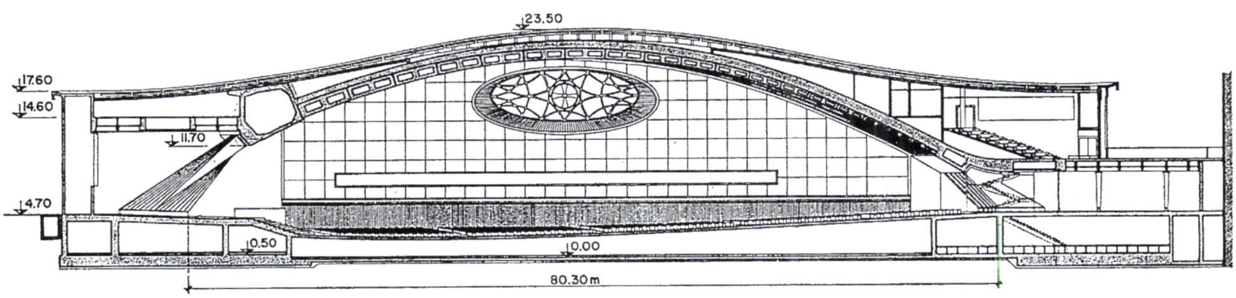
23.50
17.60
14.60
11.70
4.70
0.50
0.00
80.30 m

Projects

Palazzo dell'Acqua e della Luce

E42 (Eur district), Rome, Italy, 1939

The building was planned for the highest, most central point in the monumental E42 district, planned by Marcello Piacentini to host the 1942 World's Fair in Rome (which was never actually held due to the outbreak of the Second World War). The building was to host an educational exhibition and appear as a great symbolic sculpture paying tribute water and light. Held in February 1939, the tender for the commission had no winner, but second prize resulted in a tie between Nervi and a pair of architects, all of whom were asked to plan the project together. Nervi declined the invitation. Shortly thereafter, the war broke out and the project was shelved.

Among the various different versions of Nervi's plan for the project, the second incorporates a helical building winding around a tall tower/fountain and raised above the ground by a few bold, specially shaped pylons. The exhibition route along this rising strip terminates in a panoramic terrace overlooking the EUR district and the city of Rome.

In 1958, Nervi was once again given the opportunity to construct a building in the same area. Officially assisted by Piacentini (who, however, did not participate in defining the project), Nervi designed and built the Palazzo dello Sport with his own building firm, and it was opened for the 1960 Olympic Games.

above
Model of the building

side
Plan

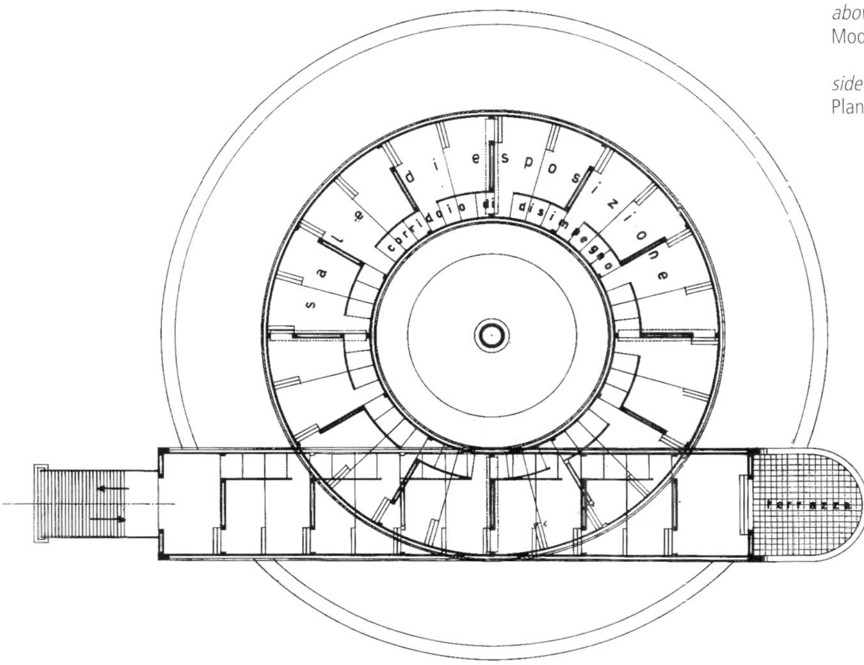

CNIT

Paris, France, 1954-1955

Details of construction

opposite page
From the top, model and cross section

In 1954, while working on plans for the Unesco offices in Paris, Nervi was consulted by fellow team member Bernard H. Zehrfuss, who, with Robert Camelot and Jean de Mailly, was working at the same time on an exhibition space for the new office district in Paris. His ambitious idea included a triangular vaulted roof resting on only three corners, with no intermediate pillars. The side of the equilateral triangle was huge, 225 metres, and there was some doubt as to whether it would actually be possible to build the structure. But Nervi was confident that it could be built and encouraged the architect to go ahead with the project.

He was later called in as consultant to contribute to the planning of the construction technique to be used.
His proposal was to divide the cross vault into three identical parts, bounded by weight-bearing arches, while the sails were lightened by a minute grid partition.
The triangular elements were to have been assembled out of prefabricated pieces on the construction site and joined together with casts to form resistant nodes (a technique he had already experimented with in his aircraft hangars). His idea was not implemented, however, and the famous building was completed using a different solution.

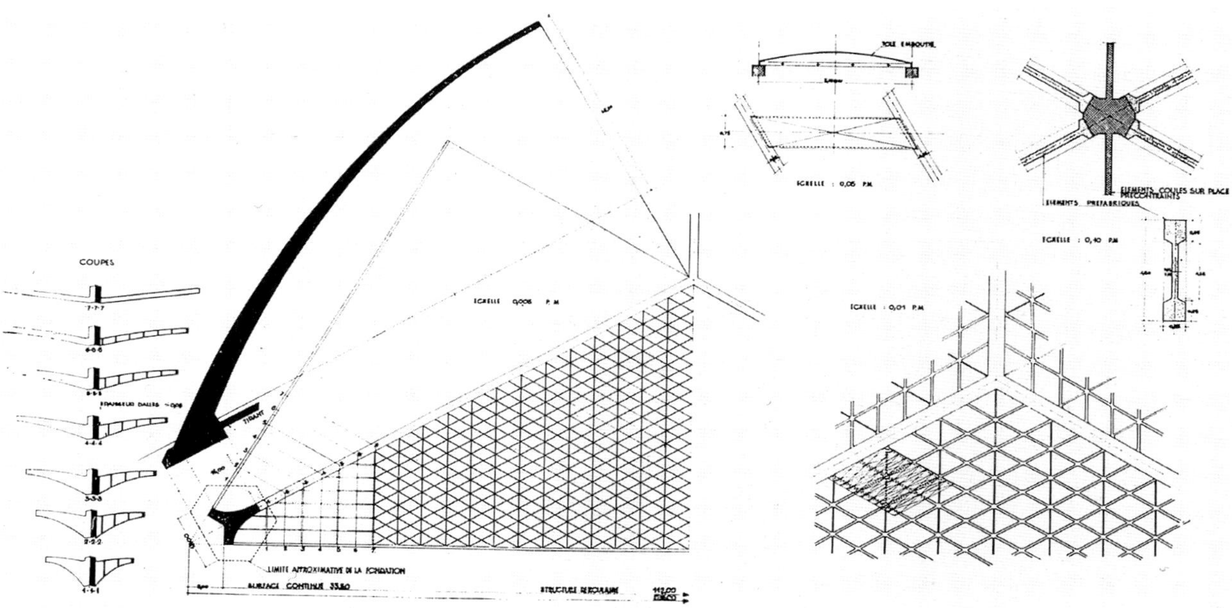

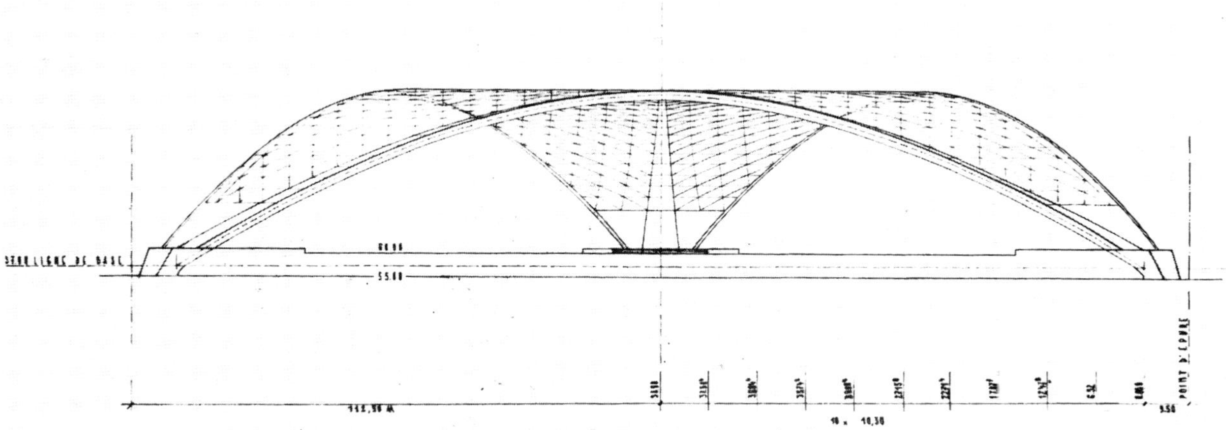

Bridge over the Strait

Between Messina and Reggio Calabria, Italy, 1969

Cross section of scaffolding

opposite page
From the top, cross section, plan and model

A permanent connection between the Italian peninsula and Sicily has been a dream since the times of the Roman Empire. When an international competition was announced in 1969, the Autostrada del Sole motorway had already been completed and its southern extension, the Salerno-Reggio Calabria road, was under construction. It seemed natural that people should be able to drive right on to Sicily. Hundreds of engineers from all over the world, who presented a great variety of suggestions: tunnels, underwater tunnels, dams, floating bridges and bridges with multiple supports. Nervi boldly proposed a suspension bridge with a single span more than three kilometres long, at a time when the longest suspension bridge in the world had a free span of only 1300 metres. Four colossal pylons with a complex shape, 392 metres high, two on each shore, placed well apart, were to support suspension cables on inclined planes, which came closer together at the centre to become tangents with the structure (with a trapezoidal section, closed by reticular girders). The project was awarded second prize in its category, but the competition was not held in view of the subsequent development of the project, which has still not been concluded.

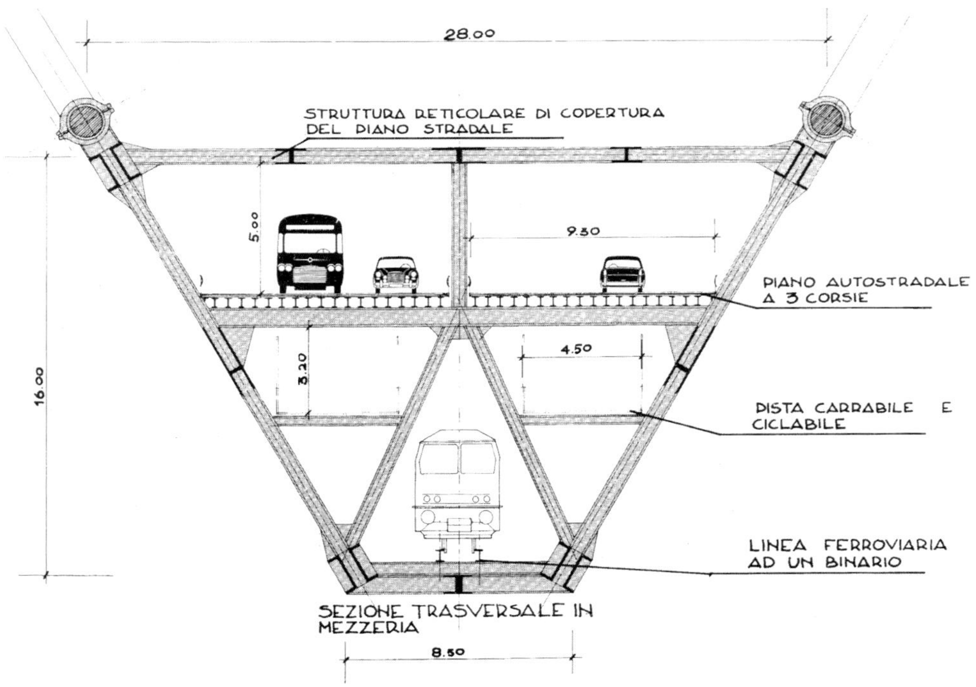

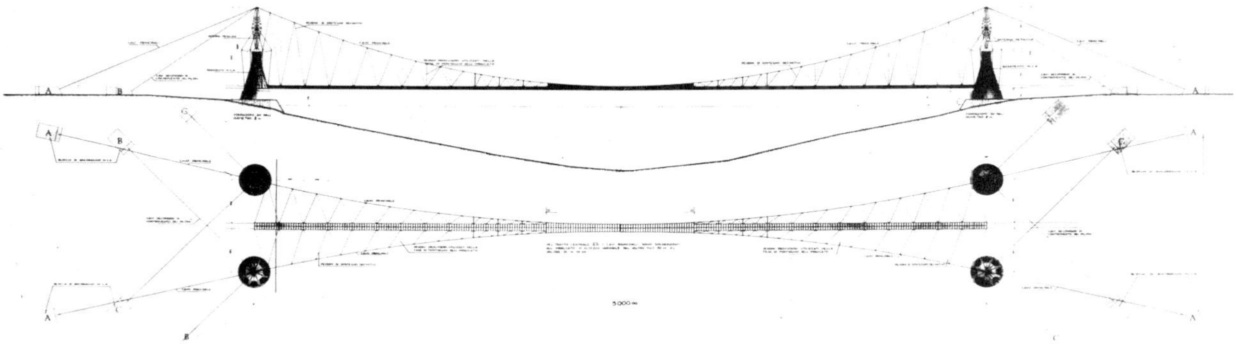

Thought

Correct Building

Technique and its aesthetic orientations

The laws of nature are the best, the most sincere, I would say, the most perfect guide that may be imagined, and having, even indirectly, introduced them in determination of so many constructions and manufactures cannot but produce excellent results. The sincerity of construction which the architect is obliged to satisfy when tackling the difficulties of a statically or dynamically important problem is the most effective school in this sort of serial, logical, I would even say honest assessment of events, circumstances and values which may give rise to an increasingly balanced conception of social life. Man, used to designing according to nature, acquires a tendency toward objective evaluation of facts, which will guide all of his other thoughts in the same way. We may therefore predict and hope that, however slowly, everything that forms the setting of our lives will be on its way to a serene functional logic that will restore every manufacture to its true essence and all social life to a higher sincerity. Nor need we fear that beauty, in the most abstract sense of the word, might be even minutely obfuscated. To the contrary, among the many changing aesthetic ideals that men have pursued over the years, the new will have the insuperable characteristic of striving to achieve a more and more complete harmony between our works and the divine laws of Nature.

P.L. Nervi, "La tecnica e i suoi orientamenti estetici", in *Lo stile nella casa e nell'arredamento*, 19-20, 1942, pp. 14-15.

The science or art of building?

Building is an art even in its most technical aspects, which involve structural stability, in that the huge complexity of the factors determining a building's static lifespan ensure that, at least at present, the accuracy of study of any mathematical or formulistic proceeding is pure illusion, the limited acuteness of which may only be increased and completed by work of intuition and understanding of static phenomena, of a personal nature which cannot be translated into absolute numerical laws.
First of all, we may say that application of theoretical research based on mathematics to the study of the internal equilibrium of resistant systems, which began in the last century and was extended until it reached its current considerable state of advancement, while it has brought formidable aid to resolving static problems, has inevitably helped dry up the sources of intuition and static sensibility, favouring that detachment between the mathematical-technical mentality and the intuitive-artistic mentality which, consecrated in the scholastic and professional division between engineers and architects, must be considered one of the significant causes of the state of crisis architecture has been in for several decades now. In this regard we may note that while for many, many centuries intuitive empiricism was the architect and builder's only guide, the grandiosity and technical perfection of many of the projects of the past reveals that, starting out with intuition alone and with interpretation of static experience offered by the day-to-day reality of building, these predecessors of ours were able to form a static sensibility, the efficacy and accuracy of which may be measured by the excellence of the works they built. This static sensibility, supreme comprehension and, I would say, almost humanisation of the inhuman laws of equilibrium and the resistance of materials, went perfectly well, due to a sort of spiritual homogeneity, with the artistic sensibility, so that the demands of construction and of aesthetics could spontaneously be combined in the architect's mind and materialise in unsurpassed masterpieces of building.

P.L. Nervi, *Scienza o arte del costruire? Caratteristiche e possibilità del cemento armato*, Rome: Edizioni della bussola, 1945, pp. 9-10.

Of certain characteristics of reinforced concrete

Reinforced concrete is the most beautiful building method humanity has managed to find so far.

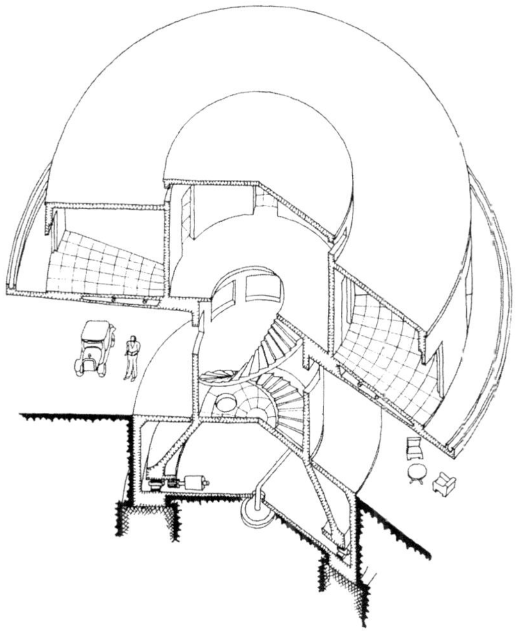

Plan for a rotating building, 1932

The fact that we can create molten stones, of any shape, superior to those found in nature because they are capable of resisting tension, has something magical about it. We have become used to extraordinary things and this has diminished our ability to be enthusiastic, but reinforced concrete still definitely deserves plenty of enthusiasm.
This material has broadened the range of our imaginations in construction practically without limits, and it is not very satisfying to see that so far these possibilities have been little explored and used. In building, and perhaps in all branches of technology, we almost always see the strange incongruence of wanting to adhere to old schemes with new procedures or materials which would have given much more significant results if used with a spirit entirely free of preconceptions.
This has been the case of reinforced concrete, which has in most cases been forced to comply with the forms and modes of resistance typical of iron, masonry or lumber, neglecting many of the multitude of possibilities offered by its qualities and its most specific properties.
We might say that the architecture of reinforced concrete is absolutely in its infancy, even though the system has been in use for more than fifty years.
The most characteristic property of reinforced concrete structures is their monolithic nature, and this is also the property which gives rise to the most brilliant specific static solutions. A girder-slab complex, even if it reproduces the older system of the wooden beams with planking over them in its outer form, differs from it largely due to its monolithic nature.
In fact the system of beams and planking, consisting of two elements, each of which works on its own behalf, is only able to resist vertical loads; the girder-slab system, on the other hand, offers horizontal resistance which, even if not required in the majority of cases, is in any case an effective, insuppressible reality.
Similarly, each girder becomes one with the pilasters on which it rests, each fabricated frame a single structure in which stress on one part has repercussions on the others and is practically diluted throughout the entire resistant organism.
If we add to this a high capacity for resistance to compressive loads, the fact that it does not deteriorate with exposure to atmospheric agents, the ease with which even the most complicated forms may be made, and, lastly, its relatively low cost, we will see that reinforced concrete is truly the most interesting, fertile building material currently available to humanity.

P.L. Nervi, *Scienza o arte del costruire? Caratteristiche e possibilità del cemento armato*, cit., pp. 77-78

Structural prefabrication

Structural prefabrication is a building procedure of great interest which has added to the potential of reinforced concrete in recent years.
It consists of building a resistant complex by connecting prefabricated cement elements so that they are statically collaborative.
Elements may be made of true reinforced concrete or ferrocement, and it will be clear what a vast

Plan for a big roof for a railway station, 1947

range of applications the combination of the two systems offers. Let me add that in both cases pre-compressed solutions further expand the range of possibilities. Apart from the technical benefits of prefabrication, it seems interesting to me to underline one of its aesthetic and architectural properties, deriving directly from two basic conditions of prefabricating systems, and that is, the intrinsic light weight of the structures produced and the speed permitted by production of elements which are all the same.
I might also point out that with prefabrication it is not particularly difficult or expensive to produce elements in complicated shapes.
A small number of templates may in fact be used to make a very large number of different elements, with the result that their impact on cost (unlike that of the usual reinforced concrete constructions, in which formworks are used once only) is of secondary importance.
The static union of different elements may be ensured by electrical welding of each segment and casting nodes of strong conglomerate.
Special treatments, such as chipping the surfaces, wetting them abundantly and applying cement mortar when casting the node, ensure almost perfect adhesion between old and new conglomerates.
One of the most delicate aspects of the prefabrication procedure is determining the proportions of the weight and dimensions of the elements in relation to the mechanical equipment which is available or may be prepared for lifting the elements and assembling them on site.
In most instances this requires careful study of the scaffolding and means of horizontal and vertical transport, the efficiency of which is the key to the success of the whole enterprise. Basically, any form of prefabrication requires much more accurate, extensive study of design than is required for ordinary reinforced concrete constructions.
I might also add that this kind of study is more difficult and delicate than one might suppose, as there are few set points of either a general or a theoretical nature, and it must be essentially based on experience, analogies and, above all, a constructive imagination which clearly foresees all

the steps involved in preparation, transportation and erection so that each of them may be defined with sufficient precision.

P.L. Nervi, *Costruire correttamente. Caratteristiche e possibilità delle strutture cementizie armate*, Milan: Hoepli, 1965, p. 33.

Experimental static research on models

It is clear that the sole aim of theoretical engineering is determining internal stress in various parts of a structure during the design stage so as to determine the proportions of resistant sections safely and economically.
But despite the accuracy of the calculation procedures used in construction science today and presumably in the near future, its ability to resolve complex static systems, particularly in the field of spatial structures, is still inferior to the creative and constructive possibilities offered by the architects' imaginations and the fertile construction methods available to us today. Steel, light alloys, reinforced concrete, ferrocement and building methods based on prefabrication or pre-compression all make it possible and beneficial to construct structures our predecessors could not even have dared to imagine, which offer the greatest promise for the architecture of the near future.
And yet it is clear that in view of the insufficiency of theoretical study for dealing with the majority of these conceivable systems, it would be impossible to make them if it were not for the fact that in recent decades we have perfected tools and methods of experimental research with practically unlimited powers of study.
It is a well-known fact that the distribution of internal stress in a structure depends exclusively on the type of structure and the way in which forces act on it, not on the metric scale of agent and resistant systems.
It follows that a model, that is, a scale copy of a structure, if subjected to a system of forces in an appropriate mechanical simulation, will find itself in a state of internal equilibrium entirely like that of the real structure.
And so all we need is equipment for reading and measuring states of stress in various parts of the model to have information on the internal equilibrium of the real structure directly (apart from the scale).
Instead of theoretically predicting the stress on a resistant complex, with inevitable approximations and simplifications, all we need do is determine them with simple direct measurement.
It is a bit like reading the weight of an object on a scale rather than using geometry to determine its volume and specific weight.
The superiority of the experimental method for studying the effective static functioning of a resistant system over any kind of theoretical procedure imaginable will be perfectly clear.
The only practical problem is the fact that making a model, subjecting it to a load and measuring stress are lengthy, expensive operations, and so it is easier and cheaper to use theoretical calculation instead whenever possible.
Research on models is limited to constructions of

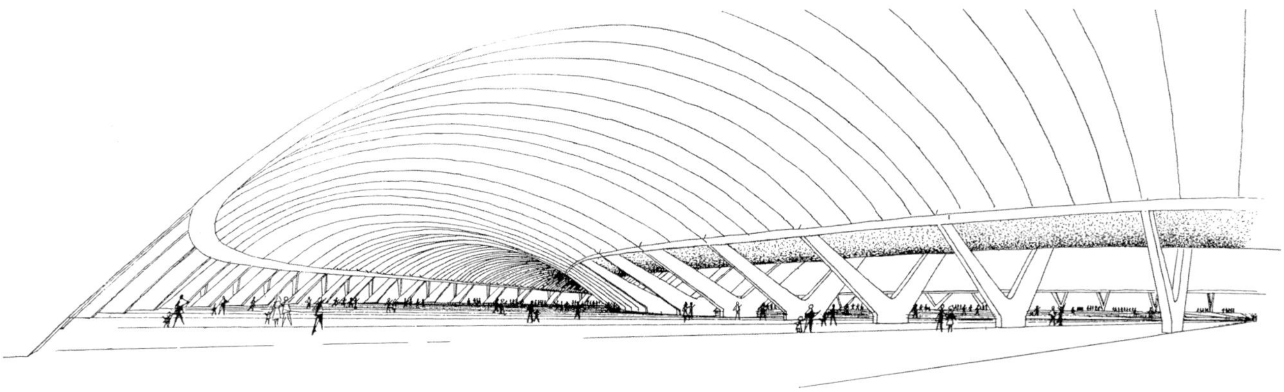

Plan for an exhibition centre in Caracas, 1956

particular technical and architectural importance and solves all the problems that escape the calculation capacity of today's construction science.

P.L. Nervi, *Costruire correttamente. Caratteristiche e possibilità delle strutture cementizie armate*, cit., p. 37.

Considerations regarding the possibilities of reinforced concrete structures

Its adaptability to any shape and ability to resist the three main sources of stress make reinforced concrete the most revolutionary material in all the history of building.
The essence of the revolution lies in the possibility of creating structures which respond perfectly to static requirements and can become the visible materialisation of the play of forces at work within them. The consequences of this go well beyond the simple technical fact, and have definitely made a major contribution to the renewal of architecture underway today. And in fact we owe the return to architectural variety, which had been lost under over-decoration, primarily to this possibility of creating structural organisms which respond to static laws and find their eloquence and formal expressiveness in this response.

With reinforced concrete even the simplest static elements acquire new expressive architectural interest. Girders lose the prismatic rigidity of wood and metal profiles and can be moulded in response to changes in inner stress; vertical supports, which are made one with horizontal structures, are no longer constrained by the uniformity of section of columns or pilasters; resistant spatial systems such as domes or vaults acquire a degree of freedom unknown to masonry structures, which were constrained by schemes that made equilibrium possible only through compressive stress.
We may, however, observe that reinforced concrete has been a part of the construction industry for more than a hundred years, and though its use has become very common in the last few decades, very few of its qualities and possibilities have been fully exploited. Apart from the invincible inertia of our minds and their unwillingness to freely adopt the new, the main cause of this delay in full exploitation of the unmatched potential of reinforced concrete is largely due to a technical consideration: preparation of wooden formworks.
Wooden formworks force concrete to fit the shapes that can be reproduced in wood, limiting the freedom of cement structures.
To this practical constraint we may add an economic one, as price increases progressively in relation to the complication of surfaces and the curves involved in them, so that many structural

elements – girders, pilasters, slabs – cannot escape the banality of prismatic shapes or flat surfaces, because of a temporary consideration regarding construction, of which no trace remains in the finished work.
The evolution of reinforced concrete architecture is therefore subordinate not only to an attitude, not yet common among architects, which does not only consider the cement structure as the most inexpensive static system but also considers it in terms of executive methods which, by eliminating the rigidity of the wooden formworks, permit economical preparation of the curved and specially shaped structures required by continuous variation in the flows of lines of force.
It is interesting to note that two orders of physical necessity which are as different and far removed as the resistance of air in aeronautics and strict response to static laws in resistant structures lead to forms which share continual plastic variability in section and curve.
From the static and architectural point of view, the most promising prospects in cement structures are offered by resistant surface systems, that is, systems in which static capacity is the direct consequence of curves or corrugations given to a surface, the thickness of which is still very small in relation to the dimensions of the whole. The efficiency of these structures is the product of their form and widespread resistant aptitude, rather than of concentrations of agent actions and resistant sections along individual elements, as is the case of the more common systems with principal and secondary ribbing.
Their full static truth will be evident if we consider that the agent actions (weights, overloads) are almost always distributed on surfaces along which they can, in the most efficient way, be diffused until they meet and balance supporting reactions.
It is of course hard to define these particular systems, which I would suggest we call resistant by form, even though nature and commonly used manufactures offer us numerous applications of them every day. The calyx of a flower, lanceolate leaves, reeds, eggshells, insect carapaces, seashells, fans, lampshades, automobile bodies, glass vases, even items of clothing such as women's hats are examples of resistance due to form, and it is definitely very important to ensure that a new form of construction will for the first time allow us to extend these structures to large and very large sizes.

P.L. Nervi, *Costruire correttamente. Caratteristiche e possibilità delle strutture cementizie armate*, cit., pp. 41-42.

Photographers

David Lees

Palazzetto dello Sport, Rome 1960
p. 94

G. Berta Municipal Stadium, Florence 1957
p. 108

Diving board Kursaal, Ostia 1957
p. 109

Sergio Poretti

Palazzetto dello Sport, Rome 2007
pp. 96-97

Kidder Smith

Cultural Centre, Norfolk 1971
pp. 98-99

Lucien Hervé

Unesco Offices, Paris 1958
pp. 100-107

South Gate
South Gate
South Gate
South Gate

CURVA
FIESOLE
BIGLIETTI
TESSERE

Critique

The Art of Building

Gio Ponti
Profile

A great Italian genius whose work rises to architecture.

G. Ponti, "Lo stile di Pier Luigi Nervi", in *Lo Stile nella casa e nell'arredamento*, 19-20, July/August 1942, p. 9.

Pier Maria Bardi
Style

Ten years ago I was in Russia, at the Moscow Stadium, with some Soviet architects. We looked up from under the tiers at the reinforced concrete structure, drawings in hand and then one of the guests said: "Nothing like Berta Stadium in Florence, that cantilever roof! Who was the architect?" I was happy for Nervi when I heard that question. [...] Nervi is one of the leaders of this generation's architecture, the man who has responded most sensitively to the invitations of reinforced concrete, definitely the engineer who developed his own unmistakable trademark in the technical heritage of this construction method.

P.M. Bardi, *Lo stile di Pier Luigi Nervi*, cit., p. 9.

Giulio Carlo Argan
Structure and space-light

And if we want [...] to resort to historical examples, Nervi's architecture can somehow be connected, on the one hand, with the problem of the "roof" as an autonomous spatial form or as determination of the limit, to Brunelleschi's research for the constructive self-support of the dome of Santa Maria del Fiore and, on the other hand, with the determination of free structural systems, to certain highly elaborate late Baroque solutions, especially those of Borromini and Guarini. These are two historic references which, it could be said, mark the first affirmation and the last, extreme, paradoxical interpretation of the "classical" rationality of architectural form. [...] The source of this constructive intuition of space is what Nervi calls static sensibility, it is what "must permit formulation and sufficiently estimate the definition of the resistant organism, independently of the use of true calculation of stability and with the aid of simple approximate calculations or very rough formulas." If we consider the architecture of Florence City Stadium (1930), and, for example, compare the weighty articulation of cement structures supporting the big inclined plane of the tiers with the spurt of the jutting roof, which curves like the wing of an aircraft, it is immediately evident that this relationship is not the result of a simple calculation of weights and resistances, of stresses and possible deformations, but reflects a much more complex and authentic sentiment of space. In the hinged spring that links this inclined plane resting on that freely jutting, slightly curved surface, two separate and complementary instances of spatial intuition find their sculptural expression: a value of articulating force and a value of rising or levitation, an abbreviated perspective intensified by the inclination and a horizon that is dilated and extended until it "covers" the whole of that perspective plane. The luminosity accentuated on the risers of the stands and the penumbra under the taut wing of the cantilever roof are nothing more than the sensible aspect, almost the landscape result, of that spatial structure. The dynamic interior is reflected in the big spiral staircases that reinforces the large elliptical ring of the stadium from the outside, with a more complex function, which is however not substantially different from that of the flying buttresses of Gothic architecture. [...] Nervi's architecture is in fact increasingly geared toward the simplest form of construction, that which reproduces the graphic purity of the design intact in reality, merely designating a limit: the roof. The aircraft hangars he built around Orbetello (1938-40), akin to large pavilions made of cement trellises, which stalled rather than supported by the flying piers, are artistically beautiful precisely because they are extended to the extreme limits of

constructability. They mark the ultimate spatial limit that can be constructed using the limit on space that can be built using equipment and technical processes currently available. Hence, they mark a limit or horizon. Only additional progress in equipment and technical processes and, therefore research in the possibilities of spatial intuition, will allow us to go beyond this formal result. It might thus be stated that the process of this technique, which continually attempts to go beyond its own results and to cast bigger and bigger arches and vaults, coincides with the artistic development of an architecture intended to include bigger and bigger dimensions within its structural coherence. [...] In more recent projects, in fact, this research is becoming more subtle, truly aiming at creating a more human environmental condition through "roofing," making room not only for a dimensional definition but for a vibrant, atmospheric and luminous substance. [...] Above all, Nervi's constructions attempt to define the structuralism of space-light; and as space-light, or space-phenomenon, which is the same thing, taking the form of a luminous sensation, it is clear that the process of formal intuition must be inspired by the sensation and aim of producing a sensation, its internal structure or consistency clearly manifested. This explains the continual variety of structural weaves in this architecture: a variety that attempts to reproduce the infinite possibilities of refraction and defraction of light rays in form, to develop all possible relationships between quantity and quality of light. The same problem of the limit, of the total resolution of architecture into the elementary principle of the roof, no longer appears to be a matter of the limit and of the relationship between indoor and outdoor space, but, rather, between indoor and outdoor light, between graduated or built light and indefinite light.
It is easy to see that precisely because of this "integral" concept of space as a light phenomenon, Nervi's architecture goes entirely beyond the traditional limit of "technical" architecture and joins it once again with the concept of space characteristic not only of all modern architecture but of the whole of the modern figurative tradition: and that is how, in this way, the severest and most scientific form of construction falls within the scope of the most dynamic contemporary figurative research.

G.C. Argan, *Pier Luigi Nervi*, Milan: Il Balcone, 1955. pp. 21-22, 25-26, 27-29, 31-32.

Ernesto N. Rogers
A Portrait

No engineer since Maillart has more realistically addressed the problem of the "tekne" in its correct, original significance.
The distinction between science and art, between use and means, represented an insurmountable divide in structural phenomena. The work of these two great engineers, Maillart and Nervi, offers a new synthesis – the very synthesis that dominated all early creative architecture and was unconscious for medieval craftsmen but then became deliberate with the Renaissance architect and his classical approach.
Seen in this light, Leon Battista Alberti's words have new meaning: "I call Architect he who, through secure and marvellous Art and Method, manages, through both thought and invention, to conceive and, with execution, to complete all the Works that, by virtue of the movement of the great Weights, and the accumulation of Bodies, can, with the greatest Beauty, be adapted for the use of Humanity."
In this synthesis the artistic vision of form and its material content need not be a dual conception generating diverging paths, but rather an intense process in which the two are interchangeable. When this process is the fruit of two opposed forces, the architect must resolve them in a synthesis.
Here the word "tekne" goes back to its original meaning. It does not refer solely, as in modern usage, to consistent interaction of technique and execution in the service of science and art but, as the Greeks used it, to a synthesis of art, science, knowledge, craft, talent and profession. This

Plan for New Norcia Cathedral, Perth, Australia, 1959

original vision of the problem naturally played a crucial role in Nervi's work as a designer and as a teacher and opened up a path leading to unexplored regions, which have thus been made accessible not only to him but to many others as well. Anyone who has had occasion to become familiar with Nervi's works and writings will know that he was sometimes a victim of his own slogans, that he was under the illusion that some of his most ingenious solutions were exclusively the fruit of an engineer's disciplined and precise mind, that the beauty in his work was due to a neutral or passive thought process that had nothing to do with aesthetics. But this illusion certainly did not blur the clarity of his thought. Nervi was an artist against his will, sometimes even against his own theoretical convictions; he is an artist because, though he possesses a staggering amount of knowledge, he does not confuse the end with the means, because he does not settle solely for the means but bends them to his purposes, using them correctly.

Nervi's typical approach to design starts on the basis of a scientific certainty but transcends it through intuition, even though his intuitive powers may be subjugated to the laws of rationality. Cocteau's formula, "First find, then look," seems to have been coined to describe the methods of this poet/engineer. If we embrace all the manifestations of Nervi's work, it will become clear that his solution to technical problems tends to define and crystallise their sculptural quality. The stylistic character of his three-dimensional language is based on study of personal expression through which form and content are identified, to the point that they become a single spatial diagram, a harmonious equilibrium between opposite sectors of thought. His special gift is expression, through mathematical rigour, of a perfect structure which, though the result of complex formulas, looks simple enough to be perceived not so much as a synthesis made by human thought as a law of nature.

Nervi's secret lies in his ability to extract and express the truth he is capable of discovering in the essence of things. He does not seek to create out of nothing, but invents his structures with the support of all the scientific and cultural developments available to us. He is like a medium who invokes the spirit of the static until it materialises; a spirit which others express only too often in terms of incomprehensible mathematical symbols. Nervi seems to say: "You try it too: it's easy, you can do it," for the relationship between thought and the creative act are so indissolubly linked in his mind, even though, in actual fact, there is nothing more difficult than expressing complicated things in simple terms.

E.N. Rogers, "A portrait of Pier Luigi Nervi", in *The works of Pier Luigi Nervi*, New York: Frederick A. Praeger, 1957.

Mario Salvadori

Sincere Structures

The truly great structures of the past are the work of individual geniuses who, practically unaided by science, were capable of conceiving and creating dreams of stone. Our age has seen the development of collaborative action in the construction sector.
The architect presents a project based on the client's wishes; the engineer analyses it to determine its stability, a process which sometimes leads him to make essential changes to the structure; the construction firm builds it, producing a more or less accurate approximation of the original concept.
Only rarely does the result of this collaboration faithfully reflect the client's original demands or the architect's dream. But even in our age of collaboration there are isolated cases of men who can boast the title of master builders, and Pier Luigi Nervi is one of the few deserving the honour of this title. [...]
If I had to explain why Nervi's structures are admired so much all over the world by architects, engineers and the general public, I would answer without hesitation: "Because they're so true."
Nervi combines the two opposite mental attitudes that are present in every one of us: the synthetic, intuitive, artistic attitude and the analytic, mathematical, scientific attitude. In him these two diverging points of view do not struggle against one another but complete one another, and their expression is characterised by such firm devotion to reality and to physical beauty as to induce use of the word truth.
Nervi's genial mind is also totally and unshakeably honest. His structures cannot but be always clear, simple and aesthetically satisfying. And, as he never tired of repeating, these results do not appear though a conscious attempt to meet certain aesthetic requirements, but address basic structural problems right from the start with the most clearly and obviously articulated static solution. Nervi says that beauty is an inevitable side effect of this search for satisfying structural solutions.
The designer-entrepreneur is under constant economic pressure: all Nervi's projects were produced as proposals in competitions for tender in which he participated with his company, and therefore his solutions also had to be as economical as possible in the context of the conditions prevailing at the time in Italy.
It should not be surprising that Nervi produced his masterpieces in a context created by these conditions. In construction as in any other art, self-imposed restrictions accepted stimulate the creator and guide him toward better results. Excessive freedom can in actual fact be a limitation on the expressive potential of a great artist.

M. Salvadori, "Foreword", in *P.L. Nervi, Structures*, New York: F.W. Dodge Corporation, 1956, pp. V-VII.

Ove Arup

At the ceremony for the presentation of the Royal Gold Medal for the year 1960

In honouring Nervi, we are not honouring just any mature engineer, architect or builder, but a man who has refused to submit to the division in the art of building. He is among the ranks of the classic builders for whom end and means come together in a single harmonious creation.
To him, purely constructive issues come first and have an essential impact on the project. This is the aspect which determines, for example, the character of the roofs with big spans for which he is justly famous. In studying the plan, he almost manages to perceive the process of reasoning and intuition that produced it.

Model for Kuwait City, 1968

The starting point is the need for economy. Beyond the tangible purpose, which is clearly a beautiful structure, a project has to be competitive; otherwise it is likely that the choice will fall on another project and another architect. When designing with reinforced concrete, it is essential, in economic terms, to direct forces toward the ground with a direct thrust, defining a dominant element such as an arch, a vault or a dome. It is equally essential to find an economic solution to the problem of the formworks, a solution that lies in repetition. This also means that a simple geometric shape is preferable for the roof, as it can be divided up into identical elements. When he is serious about something, Nervi does not allow himself to be tempted by those bizarre wrappers that are the damnation of building companies and give engineers such headaches – Nervi wants to help the building firm, not make its work more complicated. His ribbed solutions are directly derived from the formworks technique Nervi developed with so much care and intelligence: the ferrocement units that unite the ribbing and are at the same time the channels in which it is formed. The ribbed structure also ensures two very important qualities: lightness and rigidity.
Finally, of course, Nervi studies the model created by the ribbing; he manipulates it until it meets his idea of beauty, without placing too much of an accent on the economy but not starting with a preconceived aesthetic idea isolated from the construction or the structure either. The result is that his structures have that direct, inevitable quality that is undoubtedly the sign of greatness. Architecture arises out of the construction process

which, according to Nervi, is the only way of producing good architecture. [...]
The process of logical development of design which Nervi applies is, in this author's opinion, what lies at the base of good engineering and good architecture. At this level there is in fact no difference between the two; they are both the same type of activity: an activity which, even with selection and synthesis, is solidly anchored in the facts of life, such as the force of gravity or the cost of steel and labour. And I share Nervi's conviction that going too far away from this basic approach is dangerous in both architecture and engineering. It is quite natural that architects should be more exposed than engineers to the risk of neglecting the most prosaic elements of life because – as is their right – they are absorbed in the aesthetic aspects of their work. [...]
Nervi's work also represented a lesson for the engineers, who, while not perhaps as susceptible to neglecting the facts of life, risk being excessively absorbed by the analytic aspects at the expense of design considerations, and, running aground on tactical issues, forgetting broader strategic considerations. Both are equally necessary and in fact structural engineering has now become such a vast sector as to make further specialisation unfortunately inevitable. But the engineers' education does not – or at least did not – assign much importance to the aspect of conception and proportion of the structural system that Nervi rightly considers an essential part of the project. Many engineering projects, though conceived with great skill and knowledge, would benefit greatly from simple reconfiguration of their parts.
Sometimes engineers cannot understand the apparently accidental mechanism by which certain engineers become famous, if not literally praised, among architects, while other equally great engineers are completely unknown. Vice versa, people such as Maillart, whom many architects know very well, are completely unknown to many engineers. Though this may appear inexplicable, I believe it all has its own logic. Architects are interested in architecture, and therefore, what they admire in engineers is their contribution to architecture, their ability to use structural notions to expand the vocabulary of architectural expression, to produce stimulating new visual forms. And if these forms truly emerge out of the logic of structural and economic facts, as is normally the case in Nervi's structures, they deserve all the praise they get.

Hypography of the ground floor of the Australia Tower, Sidney, 1964

Ove Arup, "Presentation of the Royal Gold Medal for 1960", in *RIBA Journal*, May 1960, pp. 229-230.

Carlo Cestelli Guidi
I Remember

I even remember how, when I met him [...] he often interrupted his speech to talk about this new idea of

his, at times accompanying his incisive words by making little models with whatever materials he had at hand – paper, cardboard, plastic – which he himself used to test the resistance of forms with his hands. [...] His intuition of the static fact was accompanied by a particular sensitivity to the nature of materials. I remember that he took me onto the balcony of his studio to show me reinforced concrete elements with metal grids, which he kept exposed to the weather. In that particular way he had of expressing his enthusiasm for research, he spoke to me of "his" cemented steel, which he would have used to build boats. [...]
But I wish to close these memories of mine by focusing on an aspect of
Pier Luigi Nervi's personality, which is just as valuable to me – or maybe even more valuable – than his success as an architect.
What I mean is his human qualities, above all his modesty, which place him beyond compare: he treated every one of us with such courteous affability that we never felt the weight of his definite superiority.
I never heard Nervi boast of his successes in Italy or abroad, but I always noted the attention and interest he demonstrated when he spoke of others' work, and the way he listened to others discussing any topic.

C. Cestelli Guidi, *Memories of Pier Luigi Nervi*, speech at the meeting of AICAP members held on May 26 1979, in the C. Cestelli Guidi archive at AICAP.

Bibliography

P.L. Nervi, *Scienza o arte del costruire? Caratteristiche e possibilità del cemento armato*, Rome: Edizioni la Bussola, 1945.

P.L. Nervi, *El lenguaje arquitectonico*, Buenos Aires: Est. Graf. Platt SAC & I., 1951.

P.L. Nervi, *Costruire correttamente. Caratteristiche e possibilità delle strutture cementizie armate*, Milan: Hoepli, 1955 (2nd ed. updated and revised, Milan, 1965).

P.L. Nervi, *Nuove strutture,* Milan: Edizioni di Comunità, 1963.

P.L. Nervi, *Aesthetics and Technology in Building*, Cambridge: Harvard University Press, 1965 (English translation by Robert Einaudi).

Studio Nervi (ed.), *Studio Nervi. Progetti dal 1950 al 1971*, Rome, 1971.

G. Perugini (ed.), *Pier Luigi Nervi*, in "Rassegna critica di Architettura," 30, April-June 1954.

G.C. Argan, *Pier Luigi Nervi*, Milan: Il Balcone, 1955 ("Architetti del movimento moderno" or Architects of the Modern Movement series, edited by the BBPR group in memory of G. Banfi).

J. Joedicke, *Pier Luigi Nervi*, Milan: Edizioni di Comunità, 1957.

A.L. Huxtable, *Pier Luigi Nervi*, New York: George Braziller Inc., 1960.

H.J. Lagorio, *Pier Luigi Nervi: Space and Structural Integrity*, (catalogue for the exhibit, May-June 1961), San Francisco: San Francisco Museum of Art, 1961.

A. Pica, *Pier Luigi Nervi*, Rome: Editalia, 1969.

P. Desideri, P.L. Nervi Jr, G. Positano (ed.), *Pier Luigi Nervi*, Bologna: Zanichelli, 1979.

V. Gregotti, G. Grandori, A. Kato, G. Nicoletti, "Pier Luigi Nervi", in *Process: Architecture*, 23, April, 1981.

G. Milelli (ed.), *Eredità di Pier Luigi Nervi*, Ancona: Accademia Marchigiana di Scienze, Lettere ed Arti, 1983.

L. Ramazzotti (ed.), *Nervi oggi*, Rome: Kappa, 1983.

F. Nuti, "Opere e cantieri nel ventennio. Lo stadio comunale 'G. Berta' di Firenze", in M. Cozzi (ed.), *Edilizia in Toscana fra le due guerre*, Florence: Edifir, 1994, pp. 149-161.

C. Greco, "Pier Luigi Nervi nella tradizione delle strutture sottili in cemento armato", in *Rassegna di architettura e urbanistica*, 84-85, 1994-1995, pp. 85-97.

S. Poretti, "La Cartiera di Burgo", in *Casabella*, 651-652, 1997-1998, pp. 96-101.

A. Galluzzo, C. Battiloro, F. Varrasi, *La grande vicenda dello stadio di Firenze*, Florence: Edifir, 2000.

C. Greco, "Pier Luigi Nervi: dal brevetto Hennebique al brevetto del ferro cemento", in *Rassegna di architettura e urbanistica*, 121-122, 2007, pp. 75-89.

S. Mornati, *Lo stabilimento balneare Kursaal di Lapadula e Nervi*, Rome: Mancosu Editore, 2007.

T. Iori, S. Poretti, "Le opere di Pier Luigi Nervi alle Olimpiadi di Roma del 1960", in *Rassegna di architettura e urbanistica*, 121-122, 2007, pp. 105-119.

C. Greco, *Pier Luigi Nervi. Dai primi brevetti al Palazzo delle Esposizioni di Torino* 1917-1948, Lucerne: Quart Verlag, 2008.

T. Iori, S. Poretti, *Pier Luigi Nervi. L'Ambasciata d'Italia a Brasilia*, Milan: Electa, 2008.

Photographic references

© Akg-Images / UNESCO: 53 top
© CONI Archive, Rome: 59 top
National Archive, Rome: 23 bottom, 47 right
© Riccardo Moncalvo Archive, Turin: 42
Gianluca Capurso, Rome: 56 left
CSAC / Parma University, Plan cross section: 49 top
© Danilo Donadoni / Marka: 57
© Franck Dunouau / UNESCO: 52 top
© Lucien Hervé, Paris: 100-101, 102-103, 104, 105, 106-107
ICCD, National Italian Photographic Archive, Rome: 48 top
© David Lees / Corbis: cover, 10-11, 16-17, 18, 32, 62-63, 86, 94, 108, 109, rear cover
David Lees / Time & Life Pictures / Getty Images: 12-13
Photographic feature / L'Osservatore Romano, Vatican City: 76-77
MAXXI National Museum of 21st Century Arts, MAXXI Architecture Collections, Pier Luigi Nervi Archive, Rome: 20, 22, 23 top and centre, 24-26, 34-41, 43-45, 46-47, 49 bottom, 50, 51, 54, 55 left, 56 right, 58, 66-67, 69 top, 71 left, 72 top, 74, 75, 76 bottom, 77 bottom, 78-85, 89-92, 114, 116, 117
© Moreno Maggi / Studio Maggi, Rome: 8-9
© Truman Moore / Getty Images: 70, 71 right, 73
Sergio Poretti, Rome: 6, 14-15, 48 bottom, 60-61, 64 top and bottom left, 65, 68, 69 bottom, 96-97, 110
© Kidder Smith / Corbis: 98-99
© Andreas Solaro / Afp / Grazia Neri: 16-17
© UNESCO: 53 bottom
Pino Zac, Pratola Peligna, L'Aquila: 64 bottom right

The portrait on page 28 is reproduced courtesy of Irene Nervi.

The author would like to thank Irene Nervi and Esmeralda Valente (DARC) for their kindness and help, which made this work possible.